Celebrating your year

1975

a very special year for

_____

_____

_____

_____

_____

A message from the author:

Welcome to the year 1975.

I trust you will enjoy this fascinating romp down memory lane.

And when you have reached the end of the book, please join me in the battle against AI generated copy-cat books and fake reviews.

Details are at the back of the book.

Best regards,
Bernard Bradforsand-Tyler.

Contents

1975 Life in the USA	8
Life in the United Kingdom	13
Communal Living	18
Automotive Industry in Decline	21
Tuning in to Television	26
The Fall of Saigon	32
The Final Evacuations	34
The Fall of Phnom Penh	35
Nuclear Weapons Testing	37
US-USSR Joint Space Mission	38
To Mars and Beyond	39
IRA Bombs Britain	42
Independence and War for Angola	45
1975 in Cinema and Film	47
Top Grossing Films of the Year	48
A Decade of Disasters	49
Musical Memories	52
1975 Billboard Top 30 Songs	54
Musical Smash Hits on Broadway	57
1975 Book to Remember	59
Fashion Trends of the 1970s	60
Also in Sports	67
In Technology	69
Other News from 1975	70
Famous People Born in 1975	72
1975 in Numbers	76
Image Attributions	84

Advertisement

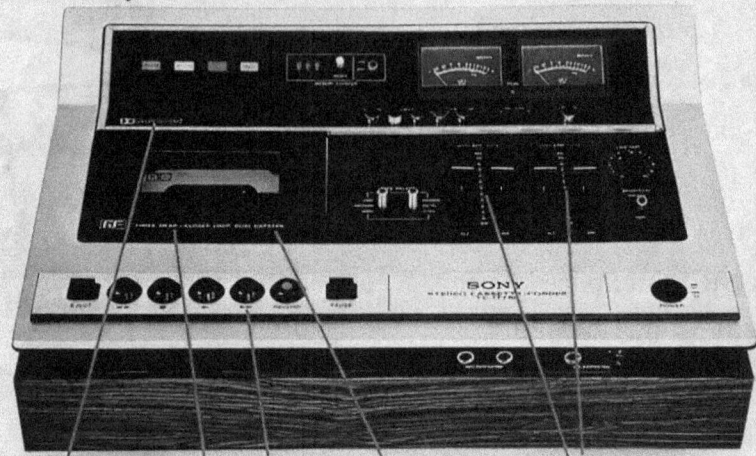

You'd swear it had 10½" reels and 15 ips.
Sony's New 3-Head Stereo Cassette Deck.
- Built-in dual process Dolby. Applies Dolby Noise Reduction to both recording and playback simultaneously for Tape/Source monitoring with signal-to-noise ratio of 63db.
- Three ferrite heads. One ferrite erase head. Two separate ferrite and ferrite record and playback heads. Inside: core and pole pieces are solid ferrite. Outside: another precisely machined layer of ferrite. Ferrite and ferrite heads last up to 200 times longer...
- 0.07% wow and flutter and at $1^{7}/_{8}$ ips. The TC-177SD features the same Closed Loop Dual Capstan Tape Drive system as Sony's finest reel-to-reel decks. Isolates the tape path in the tape head area from external vibration and abnormal tape movement...
- Professional feather-touch relay controls. Provides smooth, precise and immediate response for all tape travel modes.
- Mic/Line Mixing. Previously available in reel-to-reel only. Records two different sources simultaneously: microphone inputs and line inputs (receivers, turntables, other tape decks). Provides precise fade-in/fade-out and cross fading techniques...
- This top-of-the-line Sony goes for $699 at your Superscope dealer.

Let's flashback to 1975, a very special year.

Was this the year you were born?

Was this the year you were married?

Whatever the reason, this book is a celebration of your year,

THE YEAR 1975.

Turn the pages to discover a book packed with fun-filled fabulous facts. We look at the people, the places, the politics and the pop culture that made 1975 unique and helped shape the world we know today.

So get your time-travel suit on, and enjoy this trip down memory lane, to rediscover what life was like, back in the year 1975.

1975 Life in the USA

Imagine if time-travel was a reality, and one fine morning you wake up to find yourself flashed back in time, back to the year 1975.

What would life be like for a typical family, in a typical town, somewhere in America?

1975 was not an easy year for Americans. The Watergate Scandal of 1973-'74 caused a crisis in government, with President Nixon stepping down to be replaced by Gerald Ford. With faith and trust in government already shaken, President Ford endured two assassination attempts in September '75. Both attempts were made by young females. They were arrested and charged.

45,000 protested outside the White House, demanding jobs or income, 26th Apr 1975.

The 70's economic crisis, which began in 1973 with the Arab oil embargo, caused sky-high crude oil prices, a crash on Wall Street, rising and persistently high inflation, high unemployment and a stagnant economy, blended in a rare recessionary combination known as stagflation. It was the worst recession since the 1930s, affecting all major economies globally.

The recession effectively ended in March 1975, to be followed by years of continuous economic expansion. However, unemployment and inflation remained extremely high, well into the 1980s.

In the ten years to 1975, the US population had increased by 10% to 219.1 million.[1] Americans accounted for only 5.4% of the world's population, yet consumed a whopping 33% of the world's energy. The US economy accounted for a quarter of global production.

The Baby Boomers had become a large, vocal population of young adults. Birth rates and family sizes continued to fall, thanks to changing family values and readily available contraceptives.

Universities and colleges became breeding grounds for free-thinking, liberal theories. Students often shared accommodation, partly for cost savings, but also as an expression of a new way of living, cohabiting, exploring sexual freedoms and spiritual fulfillment.

Rock concert audience in the mid-'70s.

The hippie view of the world, with its emphasis on peace, love and nature, had focused our collective attention on the anti-war, anti-pollution, and anti-consumerism movements. Political scandals and the sky-high cost of living and unemployment levels reinforced our rejection of our parents' old traditions and conservative values. Our distrust and disgust for authority and for the status quo increased further. Environmentalists, African Americans, LGBT and other minority communities ramped up the fight for recognition and equality.

[1] worldometers.info/world-population/us-population/.

Advertisement

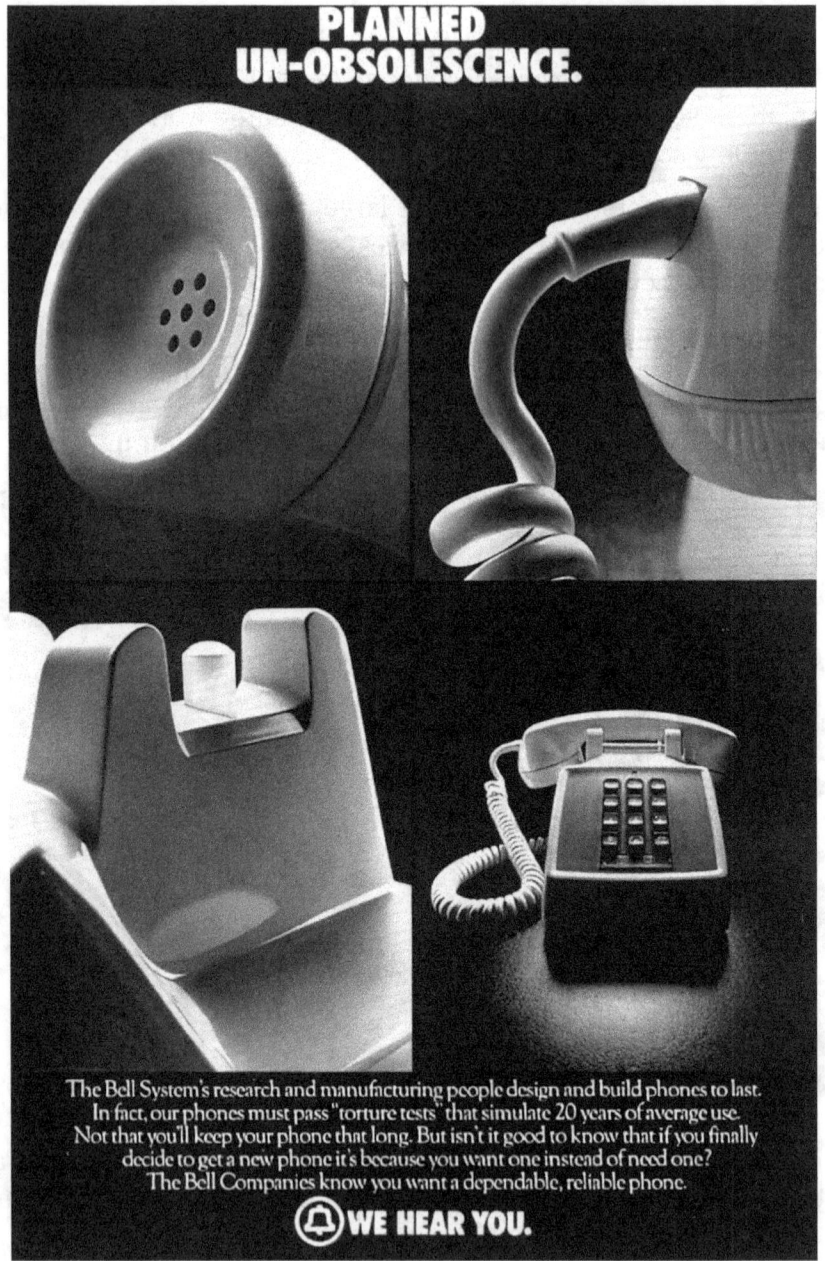

Planned Un-obsolescence.

The Bell System's research and manufacturing people design and build phones to last. In fact, our phones must pass "torture tests" that simulate 20 years of average use. Not that you'll keep your phone that long. But isn't it good to know that if you finally decide to get a new phone it's because you want one instead of need one? The Bell Companies know you want a dependable, reliable phone.

We Hear You.

At the same time, the feminist movement continued to gain momentum. Women were achieving higher levels of education in greater numbers, increasing in confidence and independence. Divorce rates were rising steeply. An estimated 50% of couples who married in 1975 would end up divorced in future years.[1]

Although the Cold War still existed between the US and the Soviet Union, the '70s saw a sustained period of "détente"—a relaxation of the political tensions between the two superpowers. Diplomatic dialogue and other bilateral agreements were reached, allowing for a substantial increase in trade between the two nations.

An event of significance showcasing the success of détente occurred in July 1975, with the first Soviet-American joint space flight. This mission marked the end of the Space Race, allowing for future joint space projects such as the construction of the International Space Station.

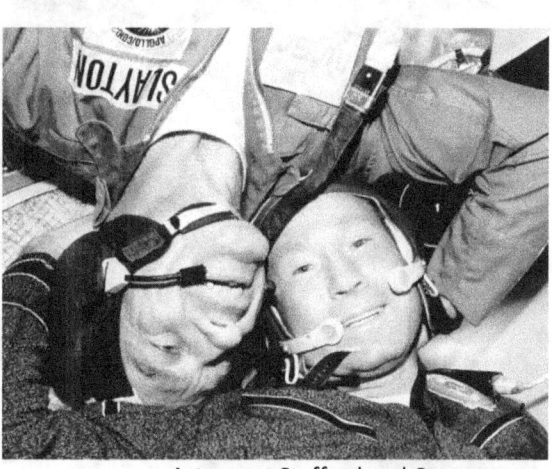

Astronaut Stafford and Cosmonaut Leonov together in Soyuz Orbital Module, 17th Jul '75.

Average costs in 1975 [4]

New house	$33,570
New car	$4,250
Color Television 25"	$569
Vacuum cleaner	$69
A gallon of gasoline	$0.72

In 1975 the median family income was $13,720 per year.[2] Unemployment stood at 8.2%, with negative GDP growth at − 0.2%.[3]

---

[1] nationalaffairs.com/publications/detail/the-evolution-of-divorce.
[2] census.gov/library/publications/1977/demo/p60-105.html.
[3] thebalance.com/unemployment-rate-by-year-3305506.
[4] thepeoplehistory.com and mclib.info/reference/local-history-genealogy/historic-prices/.

Advertisement

Only one electric portable typewriter has a snap-in cartridge ribbon.
And right now your Smith-Corona dealer can offer a snap-up price.

Smith-Corona has advanced typewriters into The Cartridge Age. We have the only electric portables with a snap-in, snap-out cartridge ribbon system.

Snap! You can replace a worn ribbon with a fresh ribbon in just 3 seconds. Or a black ribbon with any of five color ribbons.

Snap! In just 3 seconds you can replace a fabric ribbon with a carbon film ribbon that makes typewriting look like printing. You can even snap in a correction ribbon that allows you to correct errors...in 3 seconds.

Right now, we're offering our dealers this unique Smith-Corona Cartridge Ribbon Typewriter at a special low price. So if you've been thinking about a new typewriter, now is the time to snap one up.

Smith-Corona   The Typewriter of the Cartridge Age.

Life in the United Kingdom

Now just imagine you flashed back to a town in 1975 in the United Kingdom. Just as for their American counterparts, the impact of the Arab oil embargo hit hard.

The joyful, carefree optimism of England's *Swinging Sixties* could not last forever. The sentiment on the streets had shifted from frivolity to revolution. This was echoed in the music, arts, culture, and street fashion.

The country was in the grip of a three-year long recession as inflation soared to an unprecedented 24.2% and unemployment peaked at 9%. As the year progressed, the recession lifted, however the economy remained shaky. Higher living costs resulted in wage increase demands, causing an economic crisis known as a wage-price spiral.

North Shields, Tyneside residents in the mid-'70s.

The decade of the '70s was marred by continuous industrial strife, with wide ranging power struggles between the government and the powerful trade unions.

With Prime Minister Harold Wilson elected to govern a second time (1964-'70 and 1974-'76), the opposition Conservative Party elected Margaret Thatcher as their first woman leader on 11th February 1975. Within four years, she would become Prime Minister.

British feminists had a long-established history of activism and continued to grow in numbers and strength throughout the 1970s.

The newly formed Women's Liberation Movement quickly grew to become a national movement, with thousands of grassroots groups. Their list of equal rights demands included equal pay, equal education, and free contraception.

40,000 march against plans to attack a woman's right to choose, 21st June 1975.

In 1975 the average age of marriage for women was 23, and the average age for the birth of their first child was 24.[1] The fertility rate dropped to 1.8 births per woman, substantially down from the peak of 2.9 in 1964.[2] The contraceptive pill (available since 1961) and the legalization of abortion in 1967 aided in this decline.

By 1975, around 70% of British families owned a car. However, most people still relied on public transport, especially within the larger cities.

The rate of car ownership had been steadily increasing during the early '70s (around 3% growth per year). However, this growth stagnated for five years as a result of economic hardships caused by the oil crisis and recession.

[1&2] ons.gov.uk/peoplepopulationandcommunity.

By 1975, the UK was nearly half-way through repaying its post-war debt to America and Canada. The 20-year post-war building boom, which had kept cash flowing and unemployment low, was over.

Economic growth in the UK was only half that of Germany and Japan, with annual GDP having slipped from 2nd place in 1960 (behind only USA), to 6th place in 1975. Moreover, UK GDP per capita had fallen to 28th place in world rankings.[1]

By 1975, most of the former colonies of the United Kingdom had been granted independence. The cost to keep, maintain and defend them had proven too heavy a burden.

Glasgow's garbage workers went on strike in January 1975, leading to 13 weeks of rubbish building up in the alleys and streets.

Junior doctors dispute their pay and excessive working hours, with go-slows, partial strikes, and walkouts.

The "Troubles" in Northern Ireland had been raging for decades. Irish Nationalist campaigns became increasingly daring, spilling into streets across the UK as activists took to bombing targets in major cities, including central London.

Across the nation, marches, protests, riots, industrial strife and strikes were increasing. The UK in 1975 was a country in turmoil. And this was just the beginning. The worse was yet to come.

The remainder of the decade would bring a mounting series of economic crises, industrial actions and major political battles.

[1] nationmaster.com/country-info/stats/Economy/GDP.

"World Book is so easy, even my father uses it."

My father says people my age need an encyclopedia they can really use.

So he bought me World Book. He says it's just what a student needs, because it's easy to understand, and interesting enough to keep your attention.

Well, it keeps my father's attention too. Now he says it's just what a busy adult needs, because it's so interesting and easy to use.

They say World Book is for young people. But I guess grown-ups need an encyclopedia they can really use, too.

World Book. The Used Encyclopedia.

Advertisement

WHY DISHWASHERS WITH CHEAPER PRICE TAGS CAN'T COMPARE TO KITCHENAID.

They don't give you this: the powerful washing action of a full ½ HP motor. Backed by a 5-Year Warranty.* It's only in KitchenAid.

They don't give you this: a wrap-around steel frame that protects the dishwasher against hard, daily use. It's only in KitchenAid.

KitchenAid dishwashers give you features many other dishwashers don't. A Soak Cycle that even soaks and scrubs pots and pans. A three-coat TriDura porcelain enamel tub that won't scratch or fade. Thorough, forced air drying. An Energy Saver feature. And more.

See the Yellow Pages for dealers. KitchenAid, Hobart Corporation, Troy, Ohio 45374.

*5-Year Motor Warranty: If the motor should fail during the first year, it will be repaired or replaced without charge; during the next four years you'd pay only for labor.

KitchenAid
Built better. Not cheaper.

Why dishwashers with cheaper price tags can't compare to KitchenAid.

They don't give you this: the powerful washing action of a full ½ HP motor. Backed by a 5-Year Warranty. It's only in KitchenAid.

They don't give you this: a wrap-around steel frame that protects the dishwasher against hard, daily use. It's only in KitchenAid.

KitchenAid dishwashers give you features many other dishwashers don't. A Soak Cycle that even soaks and scrubs pots and pans. A three-coat TriDura porcelain enamel tub that won't scratch or fade. Thorough, forced air drying. An Energy Saver feature. And more.

KitchenAid   Built better. Not cheaper.

Communal Living

Late 1960s—Mid-1970s

By the 1970s, the Baby Boomers were young adults. Everything about them was a break-away from their parents: their music, their fashion, their values, their personal and sexual freedoms. They were non-traditional, non-conformist, anti-consumerist, anti-authority, anti-war, politically active, experimental drug users, hippies, believers and disbelievers. Anything was possible. Everything was acceptable.

The rise of communal living and "Back to the Land" movement of the late '60s and early '70s were lifestyle expressions of freedom of choice. Communes were anti-establishment and experimental. Communes were whatever the inhabitants chose them to be. Up to 3000 communes existed in the USA during this period.[1]

However, the economic realities of 1975 hit the communes hard. It was difficult to survive with the increasing costs of food, fuel, and other basic necessities. Many young adults began returning to cities to finish college. Many young couples broke up and went their separate ways.

[1] forbes.com/sites/russellflannery/ 2021/04/11/what-happened-to-Americas-communes/?sh=7454bc05c577.

Most communes encouraged co-ownership of possessions, collective chores and shared child-raising. For many, clothes, monogamy and drug usage were optional. By rejecting the 40-hour work week, many communards relied on food stamps or temporary odd jobs to keep themselves nourished.

In Vermont, a haven for hippies, an estimated one third of young adults (below age 34) were living communally.

In rural areas communards practiced living off the land, setting up farms, building their own houses, creating and selling handicrafts.

Myrtle Hill Farm, Vermont.

Communards pose in front of a geodesic dome house, Myrtle Hill Farm, Vermont. Recalls one communard, "In 1971 a young man named Bernie Sanders visited Myrtle Hill Farm... Sanders' tendency to just sit around talking politics and avoid actual physical labor got him the boot."[1]

Communards at Hog Farm, California.

The rise of communal living in the late '60s and early '70s was worldwide. Although the vast majority only survived a few years, some communes continue to exist today.

[1] From *We Are As Gods: Back to the Land in the 1970s on the Quest for a New America* by Brian Doherty.

Advertisement

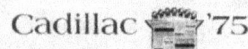

A Cadillac is no stranger to hard work.

The operating efficiency of a Cadillac makes as much sense today as it did for the businessman in the days of the 1933 five-passenger Cadillac Phaeton. Perhaps even more. And in these times, it's good to know that Cadillac for 1975 offers improved efficiency that results in reduced overall operating costs. Plus Cadillac resale...traditionally one of the highest of all U.S. cars. It's all part of Total Cadillac Value. And that goes with you wherever your business takes you. Cadillac. Then and Now...an American Standard for the World.

Cadillac '75

Automotive Industry in Decline

By the time the Arab oil embargo was lifted in March 1974, oil prices had soared four-fold, and gas prices at the pump had increased 40% from pre-embargo prices. Unfortunately, the end of the embargo did not bring with it any reduction in oil prices. The impact on the automotive industry was sustained and severe.

As the recession deepened, consumer confidence plummeted. Sales of new cars reached new lows, with November '75 figures showing an average 27% decrease from the previous year.

Traffic congestion in New York City in the mid-'50s.

Workers in assembly plants were laid off en masse. Chrysler alone placed 60,000 workers on temporary or indefinite layoffs.

About 10% of US gas stations and auto-related industries were also forced out of business.

Waiting in line for gas during the oil embargo.

Throughout the '70s, Detroit remained the car manufacturing center of America, where "the Big Three" (Ford, General Motors and Chrysler) produced the bulk of cars sold. Although still renowned for their gas-guzzling "muscle cars", consumers responded to the economic recession by shifting to more compact, fuel-efficient cars. US manufacturers were under growing pressure from the increasingly popular, more affordable and cheaper-to-run imports.

The 1975 range of American car models increased in cost, around $400 more than 1974 models. New buyers did not respond well.

American muscle cars battled to maintain relevance and dominance. These high-performance coupes with large, powerful V-8 engines and rear-wheel drive had been designed to satisfy our desire for power above all else. But clean air legislation forced automakers to drastically reduce emission pollutants. Clean air equipment became the new focus, robbing engines of much of their raw power and performance.

American auto makers responded to the stricter federal requirements, and to the increased competition from imports, by creating their own compact and sub-compact fuel-efficient car models. However poor design, inadequate engineering and manufacturing led to a string of disasters, damaging the customer experience.

1975 Chevrolet Chevy Chevette

Five car-producing countries dominated the industry in 1975: Japan, Germany, England, and France, with America in the top spot. Japan's meteoric rise into this elite group had been particularly aggressive, and their cars stood poised to dominate the world markets.

Japanese cars were compact, reliable, affordable, efficient and popular, quickly making Toyota, Nissan, Mitsubishi, Mazda, Datsun, and Honda the export market leaders. Japanese car exports increased nearly 200-fold in the ten years to 1975.

1975 Datsun 710

As we became more aware of the impracticalities and hidden dangers inherent in American car designs, European and Japanese cars were seen as more reliable, safer and more fuel efficient.

1975 Volkswagen Rabbit Golf

Advertisement

Dodge is right on target with the '75 Dart Special Edition.
It's a lot of luxury in a little car.

Dodge is right on target with the '75 Dart Special Edition.
It's a lot of luxury in a little car.

If you've found that a lot of small cars today are pretty small on comfort and style, then the '75 Dart Special Edition is the small car for you. It has an array of standard features that are usually anything but standard. Seats covered with crushed velour upholstery. Plush carpeting on the floor, halfway up the door, and even in the trunk. Map pockets are standard. So are color-keyed wheel covers. And front disc brakes. And power steering. Even the radio is standard. In other words, on the '75 Dart Special Edition, luxury comes as standard equipment.

And, as on all the '75 Darts, there are a lot of money-saving engineering features such as Electronic Ignition and electronic voltage regulator and, now for 1975, an optional fuel pacer that can help you save gas.

Today, over one million satisfied owners are already sold on Dart. The '75 Dart Special Edition is one beautiful way to make sure there'll be one million more.

Advertisement

IT COULD KEEP YOU IN THE STYLE YOU'RE ACCUSTOMED TO. FOR LESS.

Caprice Classic Landau Coupe

CHEVROLET MAKES SENSE FOR AMERICA.

1975 Caprice Classic. It could keep you in the style you're accustomed to. For Less.

If you've been buying expensive cars, automobiles with a reputation for luxury and a price tag to match, take a look at Chevrolet's Caprice Classic. It could be exactly the right car for you right now when it makes so much sense to be sensible.

Caprice offers those elegant touches you're used to. It offers all the luxuriousness any sensible person could ask for. The special combination of steel-belted radial ply tires, radial-tuned suspension and Quiet Sound insulation contributes the kind of riding comfort you'd expect in more expensive cars. And features like abundant trunk space, power steering and power front disc brakes come standard on Caprice.

And now, for those who want the latest in Chevrolet elegance—the Caprice Classic Landau. It features a padded one-half roof cover in a beautifully textured elk-grain vinyl. When you order the Landau model, you also get special pin striping and body-colored wheel covers with a Landau name, dual sport mirrors (left-hand remote operated), front and rear bumper impact strips, and the Landau name in tasteful script on the rear quarter window. The total look is that of a truly superb automobile...

Now that makes sense   Chevrolet makes sense for America.

Tuning in to Television

The television was our must-have appliance of the 20th century, taking pride of place in our family or living rooms. By 1975, nearly every US household owned a television, with 71% of them being color sets. Although color TVs had been around since the early '50s, and color broadcasts had become commonplace since the mid-'60s, the switch from black and white to color in homes had been very slow.

Outside the USA, countries like Canada and the UK were catching up with color TV ownership and broadcasting. Australia however, only began color television broadcasts in March 1975.

Elsewhere in the world, rates of television ownership lagged even further behind.

In many countries, television networks were government owned or subsidized, allowing for more focus on serious documentaries and news, without the constant concern of generating advertising revenue.

Carroll O'Connor and Mike Evans in *All in the Family* (CBS. 1971-1979).

Most Popular TV Shows of 1975

1	All in the Family	11	Happy Days
2	Rich Man, Poor Man	12	One Day at a Time
3	Laverne & Shirley	13	ABC Sunday Night Movie
4	Maude	14	The Waltons
5	The Bionic Woman	=	M*A*S*H
6	Phyllis	16	Starsky & Hutch
7	Sanford and Son	=	Good Heavens
=	Rhoda	18	Welcome Back, Kotter
9	The Six Million Dollar Man	19	The Mary Tyler Moore Show
10	ABC Monday Night Movie	20	Kojak

* Neilson Media Research 1975-'76 season of top-rated primetime television series in the USA.

Sitcoms remained ever popular, commanding ten of the top twenty highest-ranking programs for 1975. In addition, a new wave of intense TV dramas, crime and action programs were keeping us glued to our television sets.

Rhoda was the first spin-off of sitcom favorite *The Mary Tyler Moore Show*. Focused on Rhoda's (played by Valerie Harper) move back to New York, the show would welcome many guest appearances from the original *The Mary Tyler Moore Show* cast during its five-year run.

Harold Gould, Nancy Walker, David Groh, Valerie Harper and Julie Kavner in *Rhoda* (CBS. 1974-1979).

Cast of *Happy Days*: Henry Winkler, Tom Bosley, Anson Williams, Donny Most, Erin Moran, Marion Ross and Ron Howard (ABC. 1974-1979).

Airing for an impressive 11 seasons, *Happy Days* became one of the most successful series of the 1970s. The show presented an idealized version of high school life in the '50s, focused around the teenage character Richie Cunningham (played by Ron Howard) and his circle of family and friends. Although only moderately successful in its early years, the show shot to #1 after biker and minor character Fonzie (played by Henry Winkler) became a central figure in the series.

Advertisement

Introducing the RCA XL-100 ColorTrak System. TV that "thinks in color."
Its split-second "thinking" actually tracks and corrects the color signal before it becomes the picture on your screen. We challenge you to find a better color picture, on anybody's screen.

The more you know about ColorTrak, the more impressive its "thinking" becomes.

The ColorTrak System keeps face tones natural, automatically protected from the greens and purples that can spoil face tones.

ColorTrak colors stay the way you set them—light scenes to dark scenes, channel-to-channel. Picture brightness automatically adjusts to changes in room light. So pictures stay vivid even in bright light. There's a new and advanced RCA picture tube to sharpen color contrast, and enrich picture detail.

Of course, the ColorTrak System chassis is 100% solid state. And ColorTrak System sets are the most tested TVs for reliability that RCA has ever made. All the more reason, if you're buying a color TV, to see the TV that "thinks in color":

The new RCA XL-100's with the ColorTrak System.

Robert Hegyes, John Sylvester White, Ron Palillo, Marcia Strassman, Gabe Kaplan, John Travolta and Lawrence Hilton-Jacobs in *Welcome Back, Kotter* (ABC. 1975-'79).

Bonnie Franklin, Valerie Bertinelli, Pat Harrington Jr. and Mackenzie Phillips in *One Day at a Time* (CBS. 1975-1984).

The television networks were quick to turn out new programs to keep us tuning in. Here are a few of the new programs that aired for the first time in 1975: *Welcome Back Kotter, Barney Miller, Wonder Woman, One Day at a Time, Wheel of Fortune, Good Morning America* (1975-present) and *Saturday Night Live* (1975-present).

Lynda Carter in *Wonder Woman* (ABC. 1975-1979).

Original hosts David Hartman and Nancy Dussault sit on the set of *Good Morning America* (ABC. 1975-present).

Advertisement

Be a free spirit for only $2.99

Show the world you know the meaning of performance. Get the official Free Spirit Shirt. A bold red, white and blue design. Sizes to fit most everybody. Only $2.99. And only at Sears.

And while you're there, check out the high performance features on the Free Spirit 10-Speed.

Be a Free Spirit. Ride the Official Bicycle of THE SUPERSTARS. Wear the official Free Spirit Shirt. Available at most larger Sears, Roebuck and Co. stores.

The Free Spirit 10-Speed. It Performs.

Advertisement

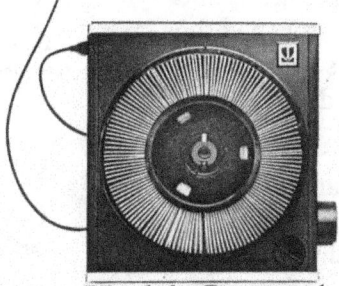

The gift that projects a beautiful image.

Good-looking on, good-looking off. That's how we designed the Kodak Carousel custom H projector series.

On duty, the Carousel custom H projector uses dependable gravity to drop each slide into place. There's no pushing or pulling. Just one beautiful slide after another.

Off duty, it has a handsome smoke-tinted dust cover that snaps on in place of the 140-slide tray. So you don't have to hide the projector away somewhere between shows.

And like all Kodak Carousel H projectors, the custom H series now comes with the $f/2.8$ Kodak projection Ektanar C lens—for a sharp projected image edge to edge.

See the Kodak Carousel custom 840 H projector shown with auto-focus at your photo dealer's for less than $227. Other Kodak Carousel projectors from less than $85. Prices are subject to change without notice.

Kodak Carousel custom H projector

KODAK GIFTS. FOR THE TIMES OF YOUR LIFE.

The gift that projects a beautiful image.

Good-looking on, good-looking off. That's how we designed the Kodak Carousel custom H projector series.

On duty, the Carousel custom H projector uses dependable gravity to drop each slide into place. There's no pushing or pulling. Just one beautiful slide after another.

Off duty, it has a handsome smoke-tinted dust cover that snaps on in place of the 140-slide tray. So you don't have to hide the projector away somewhere between shows.

And like all Kodak Carousel H projectors, the custom H series now comes with the $f/2.8$ Kodak projection Ektanar C lens—for a sharp projected image edge to edge.

See the Kodak Carousel custom 840 H projector shown with auto-focus at your photo dealer's for less than $227. Other Kodak Carousel projectors from less than $85.

Kodak Carousel custom H projectors. Kodak gifts for the times of your life.

The Fall of Saigon   30th April 1975

On 30th April 1975, the People's Army of Vietnam (PAVN) from North Vietnam, captured Saigon—the capital of South Vietnam. This brought an end to Vietnam's 30-year-long bloody civil war, and marked the start of the country's reunification under communist rule.

American involvement in the Vietnam War had officially ended in 1973 with the signing of the Paris Peace Accords. However, the terms of the settlement were not respected by either party, and war raged on, until the fall of Saigon.

With American troops and financial support withdrawn, the PAVN began their "1975 Spring Offensive"—an aggressive assault to capture the cities and provinces of South Vietnam, and to "destroy and disintegrate" the South Vietnamese troops. The PAVN captured cities and villages one after the other, during their southward march towards Saigon.

PAVN troops cross a river, Phuoc Tuy province.

PAVN soldiers pose on top of a captured South Vietnamese UH-1 helicopter at Phụng Dực Airfield.

The PAVN displayed superior organization skills in guerilla and traditional warfare. Their troops were more disciplined, with higher morale and motivation to succeed for the communist cause.

Although South Vietnam's military was better equipped, with more sophisticated machinery, its troops were thinly spread out and rife with corruption and poor morale.

South Vietnamese army outside Xuan Loc, April 1975.

The Spring Offensive in Vietnam's Central Highlands faced little pushback as large numbers of South Vietnamese troops fled home to protect their families. Villages and cities emptied in a mass exodus, a chaotic dash to the assumed safety of the coast and the south. All roads southbound became clogged in this desperate scramble to escape the approaching enemy.

Known as "the convoy of tears", the caravan of desperation continued for 15 days with no food or water available. Roads were strewn with abandoned children, the elderly, the infirm, and those who had fallen or been crushed. An estimated 40,000 refuges were shot at point blank range, intercepted by the PAVN's 320th Division.

For the survivors who made it to the coast, they faced corruption and looting from their compatriots. The PAVN were not far behind. While planes and ships transported as many refugees as they could to Saigon, millions more died, caught in the crossfire, trampled, or drowned at sea.

By early April, the PAVN were on Saigon's doorstep. Southern forces fought valiantly, while their President clung to the belief that the US would return to aid in their fight.

On 30th April, a PAVN tank smashed through the gates of the presidential palace, ending the decades-long civil war.

Vietnam's "Convoy of Tears", outside Da Nang, March 1975.

Civilians fleeing Xuan Loc, April 1975.

Captured South Vietnamese soldiers paraded through the streets of Saigon, 30th April 1975.

The Final Evacuations

29th—30th April 1975

Thousands of American citizens remained in South Vietnam after the withdrawal of US troops in 1973. In the months before the fall of Saigon, they began leaving voluntarily, and by 22nd April, 130 flights a day were flying evacuees to Clark Air Base in the Philippines. These flights included the evacuation of more than 3,300 infant and child orphans as part of "Operation Babylift".

On 29th April, the PAVN entered Saigon. All remaining US citizens were to be immediately evacuated, along with South Vietnamese government officials, embassy staff, and their families. As the airport was under siege and sea routes blocked, helicopter airlifts were the only option.

7,000 people were airlifted from the roof of the US Embassy over 18 hours as part of "Operation Frequent Wind". Helicopters landed every ten minutes, ferrying the evacuees to a fleet of waiting navy vessels.

420 Vietnamese within the embassy compound failed to secure their airlift before the PAVN tanks arrived. And outside the embassy gates, 10,000 locals clamored to be let in, desperate to join the evacuees.

From top: Evacuee helicopters approach US Navy vessels.

South Vietnamese refugees arrive on a US Navy vessel.

South Vietnamese civilians scale the US embassy's 14-foot wall.

The Fall of Phnom Penh

17th April 1975

Cambodia had endured an 8-year-long civil war when the Khmer Rouge (communist guerilla army) entered the Cambodian capitol city of Phnom Penh on 17th April 1975.

The Khmer Rouge had long been aided by China and North Vietnam. In rural areas their number and support grew rapidly thanks to resentment of government corruption, unfair policies, and anger at American bombings which killed countless civilians. The small band of guerilla fighters under the leadership of Pol Pot, had grown into an army of 50,000, most of whom supported the king, not communism.

On 12th April, "Operation Eagle Pull" evacuated US embassy staff, journalists, friendly foreigners, government officials and their families, by helicopter. Many politicians and royals chose to stay.

What followed was four years of unspeakable brutality. On the day of Phnom Penh's fall, Khmer soldiers ordered the city's two million residents into the countryside, at gunpoint, shooting anyone who moved too slow. Pol Pot was putting in place his radical plan, to transform Cambodia into a rural society. Forced to work dawn to dusk, an estimated quarter of Cambodia's population died in Pol Pot's "Killing Fields" from starvation, exhaustion, or execution.

Children were forcibly separated from their parents and placed into child work brigades.

The diary that former school official Poch Younly kept during the Khmer Rouge period describes horrendous conditions. "My body resembles a corpse, thin with only skin and bones. I have no energy, and my hands and legs tremble. No power, no strength...Everyone works like animals, like machines, without any value, without hope for the future...Why is it that I have to die here like a cat or dog, without any kin knowing of my death; to die without any reason, without any meaning?"

Cambodians toil at an irrigation project in Kompong Thom province.

Advertisement

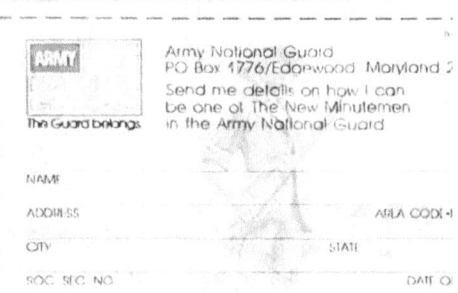

Do something different around home.

Do something different around home.

Maybe you could control the power of tons of steel.

Fire an artillery round that makes the ground shudder.

Troubleshoot your way through a maze of circuits and transistors.

You can do exciting things, one weekend a month, in the Army National Guard. You'll also learn a skill that could get you a good job. And earn extra money for things you want. See how you can have the most important part-time job in America. In the Army National Guard.

Nuclear Weapons Testing

Remember when dropping nuclear bombs was commonplace? For more than 40 years, the Nuclear Arms Race gave the USA and USSR the pretext needed to test nuclear bombs on a massive scale. Nearly 1,700 bombs were dropped by the superpowers, most of them during the '60s and '70s. A further 300 were tested by China, France, and the UK. These tests were conducted in the name of science. They also acted as a deterrent to enemy nations.

In 1975, the US carried out 24 tests, mostly at the Nevada Proving Grounds, as part of Operation Bedrock and Operation Anvil. Meanwhile, the USSR carried out 19 tests on their lands. All were underground tests, in keeping with the 1962 *Partial Nuclear Test Ban* which prohibited atmospheric, outer-space, and underwater testing.

Although most of the test sites were largely uninhabited by humans, some of them were densely populated. The effects of radioactive fallout plagued local populations for years afterward.

France remained the only country to continue atmospheric testing, ceasing in 1974 due to international pressure. The entire population of French Polynesia (an estimated 110,000 people), were affected by the radioactive fallout.

Underground nuclear test at the Nevada Proving Grounds, USA, in the early '70s.

France conducted more than 200 nuclear tests between 1960 and 1996. Fifty of these were atmospheric tests, executed over the Pacific Islands of Mururoa and Fangataufa Atolls.

US-USSR Joint Space Mission   17th -19th July 1975

The first human spaceflight partnership between the USA and the Soviet Union occurred in July 1975, when the Apollo-Soyuz Test Project brought together the two rivals. The US launched an Apollo command and service module carrying a crew of three on 15th July. The same day, the Soviets launched a Soyez 19 rocket carrying a crew of two. Two days later, the Apollo module docked with the Soyuz spacecraft while in orbit.

The main goal was to prove that two different craft could dock in orbit, using a jointly designed docking module. As the five astronauts and cosmonauts shook hands, exchanged hugs and ceremonial gifts, the seed was planted for further joint projects. For the next two days, the crews conducted numerous science and technical experiments including five joint experiments. They communicated by speaking only in the other team's language.

The countries would not partner again until the 1994 Shuttle-Mir program.

Artist's sketch of the docking of the two spacecraft.

From Left (standing): Thomas P. Stafford. Aleksey A. Leonov, (sitting): Donald K. Slayton, Vance D. Brand, Valeriy N. Kubasov.

Cold war tensions had peaked throughout the 1960s. When America landed a man on the moon in 1969, the Soviets responded by shifting their focus from the moon, to building low earth-orbit space stations. NASA and the Soviet Academy of Science hoped joint missions could potentially ease tensions between the two superpowers. They would prove that great things could be accomplished with cooperation, as long as the political atmosphere allowed it.

To Mars and Beyond

NASA's Mariner 10 made its 3rd flyby of Mercury on 16th March. Launched two years earlier, it was the first spacecraft to explore two planets in a single mission, flying past Mercury and Venus, transmitting back thousands of images of both planets. Last contact was made on 24th March 1975, after which the spacecraft exhausted its nitrogen maneuvering gas supply.

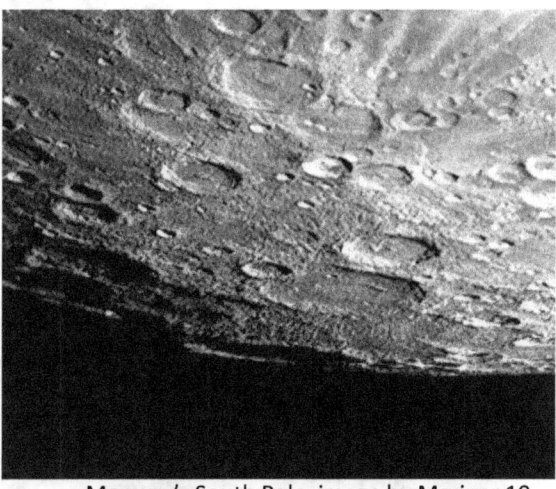

Mercury's South Pole, image by Mariner 10.

On 8th June 1975, the Soviets launched Venera 9 on a mission to Venus. The spacecraft began transmitting on 20th October 1975—the first images to be sent from the surface of another planet.

NASA Technicians working on the heatshield of Viking 1's lander prior to launch, 1st July 1975.

On 20th August 1975, NASA launched Viking 1 on an 11-month cruise to Mars. It was followed by Viking 2 on 9th September 1975. Each had an orbiter and a lander, and would become the first two spacecraft to land on Mars. They beamed high-resolution images back to earth, searched for signs of life, and analyzed the composition and structure of the planet's atmosphere and surface using robotic arms and onboard laboratories. Transmissions continued until 1982.

Advertisement

If the picture's worth taking, it's worth good processing.

Taking a good picture doesn't just depend on who takes it—and with what. Processing can make a world of difference. And that's why it's so important to choose a quality processing service. Someone who can make the picture worth the taking. So, when you leave your Kodak color film for developing, ask your dealer for quality service by Kodak or one of the many other quality photofinishers.

A message from Eastman Kodak Company on behalf of photo dealers and finishers.

The all 747 airline across the North Atlantic and Pacific.

According to the most recent survey by the Airline Passengers Association, an overwhelming majority of world travelers who answered chose the 747 as the plane they most preferred to fly. According to the same survey, Pan Am was the airline they most preferred to fly, when traveling abroad. Maybe it's that Pan Am flies more 747s to more places in the world than any other airline.

Pan Am — America's airline to the world.

IRA Bombs Britain

17th -19th July 1975

The 30-year-long nationalist campaign in Northern Ireland, known as *The Troubles*, peaked in the early '70s as Roman Catholic Republicans (IRA) fought against Protestant Ulster Unionists and the British military. Although often mistaken for a war of religion, *The Troubles* was in fact a political war. The Republicans were fighting for the reunification of Northern Ireland with the Republic of Ireland. The Unionists sought to keep Northern Ireland as part of the UK.

British troops patrolled Northern Ireland's streets for 37 years. Although their role was officially neutral, they were condemned for covertly supporting the Unionists, and were permitted to imprison IRA suspects without trial.

In the early 1970s, the Provisional IRA (militant faction of the IRA) expanded its Mainland Campaign, bringing their terror to the streets of Britain. They exploded bombs in central London and other major cities, on high streets, public transport, department stores, hotels, crowded pubs and restaurants. In addition, high profile individuals were attacked and assassinated.

A total of 21 miles (34 km) of Peace Walls were built in Northern Ireland to physically separate Republicans from Unionist neighborhoods. In recent years these walls have become something of a tourist attraction.

The damaged front of Scott's Oyster Bar following an IRA bombing, 12th Nov 1975.

From 22nd Dec '74 to 17th Jan '75, the IRA observed a ceasefire, to allow the British government time to respond to proposals jointly prepared by the IRA and Protestant clergymen. Days after the end of the ceasefire, the IRA attacked two London hotels and a pumping station in North London.

On 27th Jan, the IRA exploded five bombs across London and one in Manchester. These included the busy shopping precincts of Old Bond Street, Kensington High Street and Victoria Street. A further two bombs in Hampstead and Putney were defused.

An IRA bomb exploded in the military outfitters Gieves, 27 Old Bond Street, London W1, 6.30 pm on 27th Jan '75.

A new ceasefire began on 10th Feb '75 and would last until 23rd Jan '76—the longest ceasefire up to then. Despite the ceasefire, attacks by the IRA and Protestant Unionists continued across Northern Ireland and England, with multiple casualties on both sides.

On 5th Dec 1975, the policy of "Interment" came to an end. Begun in 1971, Internment allowed the British Army operating in Northern Ireland the right to arrest and imprison without trial, anyone suspected of being involved with the IRA.

Nearly 2,000 people were interned during this period, subject to interrogation using methods described by the European Commission of Human Rights in 1976 as torture.

A suspected Republican rounded up for internment in 1971. During the first four days of legalized Internment, violence erupted resulting in 20 civilian deaths.

Advertisement

Colors you could never get before in 60 seconds.

Our remarkable Super Shooter Land camera uses 6 different kinds of instant picture film—and the most dramatic is our new Type 108 Polacolor 2.

Special metallized dyes (the same dyes we developed for the SX-70) now give your 60-second pictures amazing new brilliance. You get more red, more blue, more yellow and more green than ever before.

And the Super Shooter comes with an electric eye and electronic shutter for automatic exposures, 3-element focusing lens and a built-in flashcube attachment. And $25 gets it all.

Polaroid's $25* Super Shooter for the new Super Colors.

Colors you could never get before in 60 seconds.

Our remarkable Super Shooter Land camera uses 6 different kinds of instant picture film—and the most dramatic is our new Type 108 Polacolor 2.

Special metallized dyes (the same dyes we developed for the SX-70) now give your 60-second pictures amazing new brilliance. You get more red, more blue, more yellow and more green than ever before.

And the Super Shooter comes with an electric eye and electronic shutter for automatic exposures, 3-element focusing lens and a built-in flashcube attachment. And $25 gets it all.

Polaroid's $25 Super Shooter for the new Super Colors.

Independence and War for Angola 11th November 1975

The cost for Portugal to maintain control over its African colonies had exacted a heavy financial toll on its economy. Up to 40% of the country's budget was being spent annually fighting the "War of Liberation" in Angola, Guinea-Bissau and Mozambique. Following a military coup ending Portugal's decades-long fascist dictatorship, its new government promptly ended the unpopular and expensive war.

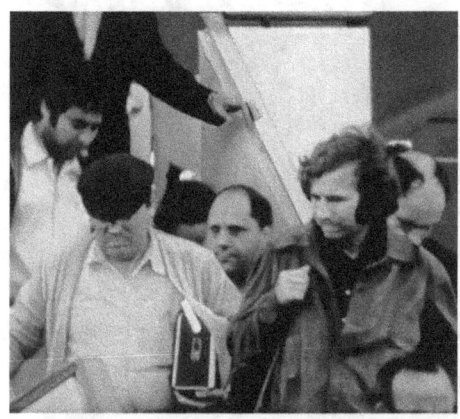
Portuguese returnees from Angola, 1975.

Half a million "returnees", mostly white Portuguese settlers, arrived in Lisbon during 1974-'75. They were offered assistance with food, finance and accommodation. However, many returning families had lived in Africa for generations, and most had never set foot in Portugal before. Far from returning home, they felt like refugees. They had been forcibly removed from their comfortable and prosperous lives as the colonizer, settler minority.

Portugal withdrew from Angola without supervising any elections or ensuring a peaceful transition. There was no formal handover of power. The Portuguese Military and civilian settlers simply fled.

Angola was granted independence on 11th Nov 1975, ending its 13-year-long guerilla war with Portugal and marking the start of a violent civil war which would last 27 years.

Two former anti-colonial guerrilla movements battled for power, with one side gaining support from the Soviets and Cuba, and the other securing assistance from the USA and South Africa. Angola had became a Cold War battleground.

During the next 27 years of fighting, up to 800,000 people would die and over one million Angolans would become internally displaced.

Cuban and Angolan soldiers weapons practice.

Advertisement

Honda has a bike for the both of you.

The exciting MT-250 K1. The quick-change artist. One minute, you're Mr. All-Business. Next, a snarling rough rider. It comes naturally on this sleek descendant of the famous race-winning Honda CR's.

You've got ample power. A 248cc single-cylinder, two-stroke engine. A six-port design with automatic oil injection. You've got the flexibility of an on/off-road type five-speed transmission. The welcome comfort of a suspension you can adjust, both front and rear. You'll like the way the rakish handlebars with CR-type grips fit your hands. And the styling! Drama on wheels. Clean lines. Rich metallic silver paint. Fine chromed accents. The MT-250 K1 comes fully equipped. Street-legal. With the latest safety refinements. All in all, the bike that fits where you are...

Honda   Good things happen on a Honda.

1975 in Cinema and Film

As cinema-goers, our interests and focus had shifted away from traditional classic Hollywood standards, which were often bounding with optimism and happy endings. We were seeking movies that reflected the political and social changes and controversies of the times, offering more depth, more pain and a sense of reality.

By 1975, a new breed of directors including Francis Ford Coppola, Martin Scorsese, Stanly Kubrik and George Lucas, demanded more artistic control. They bravely tackled darker, more gritty, pessimistic themes of war, crime, depression and inner turmoil.

A new generation of more versatile character actors rose to replace the retiring golden-era stars. Robert De Niro, Meryl Streep, Dustin Hoffman, Jack Nicholson, Al Pacino, and Harvey Keitel are some of our enduring favorites.

Jack Nicholson as "Mac" McMurphy in *One Flew Over the Cuckoo's Nest*, (United Artists, 1975).

The era of cinema houses owning their actors and controlling their directors had ended. Artists could now be represented by The Creative Artists Agency (founded in 1975).

John Travolta in 1983.

1975 film debuts

Carrie Fisher	Shampoo
Richard Gere	Report to the Commissioner
Sam Neill	Landfall
Dennis Quaid	Crazy Mama
Patrick Stewart	Hennessy
John Travolta	The Devil's Rain

* From en.wikipedia.org/wiki/1975_in_film.

Top Grossing Films of the Year

1	Jaws	Universal	$133,400,000
2	One Flew Over the Cuckoo's Nest	United Artists	$59,200,000
3	The Rocky Horror Picture Show	20th Century Fox	$50,420,000
4	Shampoo	Columbia	$23,822,000
5	Dog Day Afternoon	Warner Bros.	$22,500,000
6	The Return of the Pink Panther	United Artists	$20,017,000
7	Three Days of the Condor	Paramount	$20,014,000
8	Funny Lady	Columbia	$19,313,000
9	The Other Side of the Mountain	Universal	$18,012,000
10	Tommy	Columbia	$17,793,000

* From en.wikipedia.org/wiki/1975_in_film by box office gross in the USA.

Steven Spielberg's heart-stopping thriller *Jaws*, became the highest-grossing movie of all time. It set the standard for summer blockbusters, with millions spent on pre-release advertising. TV spots exploited the intensely suspenseful score by composer John Williams, sending audiences flocking to the cinemas on the opening weekend. The film recouped its production costs within ten days.

Miloš Forman's psychological drama *One Flew Over the Cuckoo's Nest* saw Jack Nicholson as a patient in a mental institution. The many deeply troubling scenes and themes gave critics and audiences much to debate. The film won all five major Academy Awards (Best Picture, Actor, Actress, Director, and Screenplay).

A Decade of Disasters

Airport 1975, (Universal Pictures, 1975).

The Towering Inferno (20th Century Fox, 1974).

The decade of the '70s saw the disaster movie genre reign supreme at the box office. Large casts, multiple plot lines, life or death calamities and impossible tales of survival kept us on the edge of our seats.

Earthquake (Universal, 1974).

The Hindenburg (Universal Pictures, 1975).

Advertisement

Introducing the precision of Technics direct-drive for under $200.

Technics SL-1500 has a lot more going for it than just its price tag. It also has the Technics direct-drive system. The same direct-drive system many radio stations are using in other Technics turntables.

Unlike conventional turntables, the SL-1500 has no belts or idlers to produce variations in speed. Because its platter is actually a part of the motor (an extension of the rotor shaft). So, like all of our manual turntables, the SL-1500's wow and flutter is an incredibly low 0.03%.

The SL-1500 has a DC motor that spins at exactly 33 or 45 rpm. And, unlike rumble-producing high-speed motors, the SL-1500's motor introduces so little vibration that any rumble remains inaudible (-70 dB DIN B). And the motor is electronically controlled. So fluctuations in AC line voltage have no effect on turntable speed.

There's a gimbal-suspended S-shaped tone arm with four pairs of pivot bearings to enhance its rotational sensitivity. And a $9^1/_{16}$" pivot to stylus length. For outstandingly low tracking error. The SL-1500 also has viscous damped cueing and variable pitch controls. One anti-skating adjustment for all types of styli. CD-4 phono cables. It even comes with a base and a detachable hinged dust cover.

So if you've wanted a Technics direct-drive turntable but thought you couldn't afford one, audition the Technics SL-1500. It's the turntable you've been waiting for. The concept is simple. The execution is precise. The performance is outstanding. The name is Technics.

Advertisement

Billy Preston's Bently has the best sound in car stereo.
And Billy Preston knows sound.

Billy says it's almost like riding in a sound studio.
   That's because Craig Powerplay has three times the power of conventional car stereo. And more power means clearer sound with less distortion at all listening levels. There are six cassette or 8-track models to choose from.
   You'll know great sound too when you hear Billy's latest, "It's My Pleasure" on Crag Powerplay.

Musical Memories

The music scene in 1975 was arguably more confused, complex, and inspirational than any other year before it. A wide mix of genres competed for dominance. Country, easy listening, pop, hard rock, heavy metal, disco and soul music all gained #1 Billboard placings.

On the airwaves, commercial radio stations brought us a curated playlist of the latest song releases, encouraging us to rush out and buy our preferred artist's single or album to help push them up the charts.

Multiple career-defining albums were released in the year 1975.

Pink Floyd's *Wish You Were Here* explored themes of alienation, loneliness, and mental health. The haunting 5-song album became one of the most influential and best-selling of all time.

Born to Run—the third studio album for Bruce "The Boss" Springsteen—established the artist as a noteworthy singer-songwriter. With his signature raspy voice, his lyrics often championed the social struggles of the working class.

In October, both *Time* ("Rock's New Sensation") and *Newsweek* ("Making of a Rock Star") featured Springsteen on their cover.

Queen's *A Night at the Opera*, was a wildly experimental and monumental album. Weaving between genres, the band fused together ballads, progressive rock, pop and opera styles. The epic six-minute first single *Bohemian Rhapsody* became an instant world-wide hit.

Elton John released two studio albums in 1975—*Captain Fantastic and the Brown Dirt Cowboy* and *Rock of the Westies*. Both debuted at #1 on the US charts—the first albums ever to do so.

1975 also saw the glam rock singer star in the film adaptation of *Tommy* (Colombia Pictures), receive a star on the Hollywood Walk of Fame, and be named *Outstanding Rock Personality of the Year* at the Rock Music Awards.

Disco peaked in the mid-'70s, with the first disco hits charting at #1 in 1975. From the counterculture dance clubs of the early '70s, disco emerged as an escape from the political and economic depressions of the era. Radio stations began playing non-stop disco segments, while record shops sold Disco Party LP mixes.

Below: The Bee Gees and Donna Summer.

The Bee Gees and Donna Summer ruled as Kings and Queen of disco. While we were grooving to *You Sexy Thing* (Hot Chocolate), *The Hustle* (Van McCoy), *Lady Marmalade* (Labelle), and *I Will Survive* (Gloria Gaynor), Motown joined in the disco fever. The Supremes, Gladys Knight and the Pips, The Temptations and The Jackson 5 were just some of the Motown acts taking up disco beats.

Disco's up-tempo heavy rhythms came with energetic dance moves and glitzy fashions in the nightclubs, where race and sexual orientation became irrelevant. Club DJs began making a name for their "art" by mixing tracks and adding in reverb and other effects. Club drugs such as "poppers", "speed" and Quaaludes were dance floor favorites.

1975 Billboard Top 30 Songs

	Artist	Song Title
1	Captain & Tennille	Love Will Keep Us Together
2	Glen Campbell	Rhinestone Cowboy
3	Elton John	Philadelphia Freedom
4	Freddy Fender	Before the Next Teardrop Falls
5	Frankie Valli	My Eyes Adored You
6	Grand Funk Railroad	Some Kind of Wonderful
7	Earth, Wind & Fire	Shining Star
8	David Bowie	Fame
9	Neil Sedaka	Laughter in the Rain
10	Eagles	One of These Nights

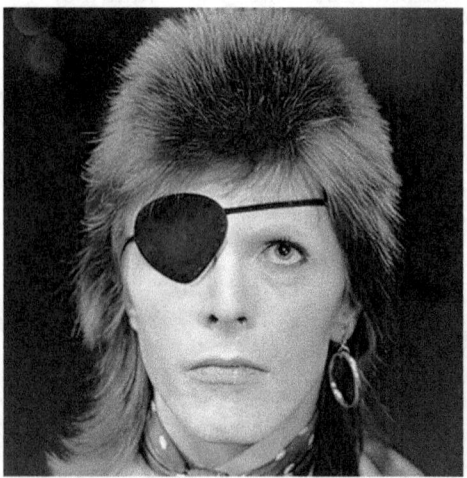

David Bowie, 1974.

The Eagles, 1975.

Captain and Tennille, 1976.

Stevie Wonder.

	Artist	Song Title
11	John Denver	Thank God I'm a Country Boy
12	Bee Gees	Jive Talkin'
13	Eagles	Best of My Love
14	Minnie Riperton	Lovin' You
15	Carl Douglas	Kung Fu Fighting
16	The Doobie Brothers	Black Water
17	Sweet	The Ballroom Blitz
18	B.J. Thomas	(Hey Won't You Play) Another Somebody Done Somebody Wrong Song
19	Tony Orlando and Dawn	He Don't Love You (Like I Love You)
20	Janis Ian	At Seventeen

John Denver, 1975.

Helen Reddy, 1973.

	Artist	Song Title
21	Average White Band	Pick Up the Pieces
22	Van McCoy & the Soul City Symphony	The Hustle
23	Labelle	Lady Marmalade
24	War	Why Can't We Be Friends?
25	Major Harris	Love Won't Let Me Wait
26	Stevie Wonder	Boogie On Reggae Woman
27	Freddy Fender	Wasted Days and Wasted Nights
28	Helen Reddy	Angie Baby
29	The Isley Brothers	Fight the Power
30	Ozark Mountain Daredevils	Jackie Blue

* From the *Billboard* top 30 singles of 1975.

Advertisement

There's not a wasted inch of space. Top, sides and front. Switches, toggle switches and dials. Sony technology has mastered the portable radio. Here's a list of things this radio can do.

First, and most important, it makes a tremendous sound. Only 8" high, the speaker is an oversized $4^3/_4$". That's backed up by a powerful 2.8-watt (max.) output. And that's backed up by a "Squelch Switch" to suppress interfering noise. So what you end up with are the rich velvety tones that normally come out of radios too big to carry around.

There are three bands, FM, AM, and Public Service (Police car transmissions, for instance.) A "moving film" style tuning dial. And a 60-minute timer that turns the radio on and off.

Why not stop in at a Sony dealer and get checked out. Then find a lonely stretch of road, and open her up.

The Cockpit. "It's a Sony."

Musical Smash Hits on Broadway

Two of musical theater's greatest Broadway shows debuted in 1975. *Chicago* opened on 3rd June at the 46th Street Theatre. *A Chorus Line* opened on 25th July at the Shubert Theatre. Both musicals quickly became Broadway and international sensations.

Packed with one show-stopping number after another, intense dance sequences, emotional characters and engaging plots, both shows told stories of dancers and singers vying for success in the spotlight.

Chicago initially ran for 936 performances, closing in 1977. It was revived in 1996 and has never closed, making it the longest-running American musical in Broadway history.

Jerry Orbach and Gwen Verdon, in the original Broadway production of *Chicago*.

Set in the razzle-dazzle of the roaring twenties, the original show was directed and choreographed by Bob Fosse with Chita Rivera and Gwen Verdon in the lead roles.

A 2002 film adaptation won six out of thirteen Academy Award nominations, including the top award for *Best Picture*.

A Chorus Line ran for 6,137 performances, becoming the longest-running production in Broadway history at that time. The musical focused on the hopes and dreams of 17 multi-ethnic dancers auditioning for a spot in a stage show chorus line.

A Chorus Line was an immediate critical and box office success, winning nine out of twelve Tony Award nominations. *Chicago* was nominated for eleven Tony Awards, but failed to win any due to its rival's dominating success.

New from Wella. Herbal Blossoms Shampoo.
It leaves your hair as clean and fragrant and beautiful as fresh blossoms.

It's excitingly new, this unforgettably fragrant shampoo from Wella. A gentle blend of delicate herbs and sweet fragrant blossoms.

Wella Herbal Blossoms Shampoo is made with organic conditioning ingredients and is pH controlled. Its rich lather leaves your hair feeling as it never has before.

Gloriously fresh and clean, as alive and fragrant as a fresh flower. Full of shine, bounce and body.

To create this beautiful shampoo, we gathered camomile, clary sage and thyme from gentle sloping meadows and spruce from deep forests. We followed the nostalgic scent of jasmin and mimosa to places where they spill over garden walls and cool pools of summer rain. And from quiet sun-warmed valleys we added nature's sweetest violets and most delicate carnations.

All for you, from Wella. New Herbal Blossoms Shampoo...

1975 Book to Remember

The list of outstanding and memorable books hitting the shelves in 1975 is long and notable. Many have gone on to become literary classics, inspiring TV or film adaptations and spin-off books. Here are some of the new releases that you may have read, or at least heard about: *Salem's Lot* by Stephen King, *Shōgun* by James Clavell, *Ragtime* by E.L. Doctorow, *The Eagle Has Landed* by Liam Devlin, *Terms of Endearment* by Larry McMurty, *The Great Train Robbery* by Michael Crichton, *All Things Bright and Beautiful* by James Herriot, *The Moneychangers* by Authur Hailey, *The Autumn of the Patriarch* by Gabriel Garcia Marquez and *Animal Liberation* by Peter Singer.

Fashion Trends of the 1970s

By the early '70s, the fashion industry had lost its way, with designers and consumers alike seeking new directions and answers to the changing times. This was a decade without guidance and without rules. Trends caught on and shifted quickly. Fashions were varied and experimental. Pants got wider, skirts got shorter, and boots got taller. And within a season the trends reversed. Anything was possible, everything was acceptable.

Walking down any street you would have found skirts worn mini, midi, or full length. Pants could be slim-fit, wide, or bell-bottomed, hip-hugging or waist-clinching. Tops might be tie-dye swirl-patterned or bold solids. Shirts came long and loose, or tight and tailored.

Daywear pants-suit and skirt-suit.

Dresses came in all shapes and lengths too. They could be short Mod shifts, or calico lace prairie-style. They could be tailored with shirt-style collars and buttoned-down fronts. They could be long and loose caftans, flowing maxi-dresses, or waisted tailored-cut with belts and A-line skirts taken straight from the '50s.

Patchwork maxi-dresses by Yves Saint Laurent.

The hippie and psychedelic fashions were adopted and modified by mainstream non-hippies into more elegant structured forms. Caftans, prairie dresses, patchwork fabrics, shawls, tassels and beads hit the runways, and the streets, in the early '70s.

Elizabeth Taylor during her bohemian period, 1969.   Maudie James models Thea Porter patchwork dress, 1970.   Weipert and Burda fashion show, 1972.

In contrast to the hippie trends, Mod dresses of the early '60s made a comeback. Space-age synthetics and plastics, widely used in the '60s, were replaced with comfortable cottons and stretch knits. In winter, tunic dresses could be worn over turtlenecks, with woolen stockings or thigh-high boots.

Mod mini dresses worn with white boots or shoes, early 1970s.

The '70s were the first full decade where pants for women gained mainstream acceptance, and we couldn't get enough of them. Pants could be worn for any occasion—pants-suits for the office, silky patterns for evenings, or blocks and geometrics dressed down for daywear. And let's not forget blue jeans, the staple of casual wear for both men and women.

Day wear pants from the Sears Spring/Summer catalog, 1970.

In the early '70s men and women wore their pants gently flared at the base. As the decade progressed, the flares got wider and wider, exploding into bell-bottoms by the mid-'70s.

Embroidered denim. Flared knit polyester pants. Flared silky jumpsuits.

Advertisement

New Dingo Brigade. Like nothing else.

Now. A real down-to-earth boot. In leather that feels butter smooth, but has the muscle to keep on going. The new Dingo Brigade Collection. With double leather soles. Stacked leather heels. And a great fit that goes right down to the all-new frontier toe. The price is down-to earth, too. Because with Dingo, you get more boot for less bucks.

Dingo. We also make Acme Western boots.

Shiny polyester Nik Nik shirts.   Stretch polyester.   Terry toweling jumpsuits.

Caught between the hippie and mod fashion extremes, the rest of us settled for easy-care. Whether it was casual, formal or business attire, being easy to wash and drip-dry dictated what we wore. Non-iron wool jersey knits and non-iron polyester were the material of choice for men and women throughout the '70s.

The '70s are often considered to be the decade that fashion forgot (or the decade of fashion that we would rather forget). And it's not hard to see why. Anything and everything became acceptable, no matter how outlandish or mismatched.

Here are some of our more questionable fashion decisions from the decade.

Shiny stretch polyester jumpsuits.   Denim on denim.   Stretch knit pantsuits.   Safari suits.

John Travolta in *Saturday Night Fever* (Paramount Pictures, 1977).

Dancer at Studio 54, New York.

And then there was disco.
It shone so brightly. It glittered so briefly.
And in a flash, it was gone.

Sporting silver lamé jumpsuits.

Dancers at Studio 54, New York.

Model wears sequined jumpsuit.

Advertisement

Bush Jacket Jean Suit—What a combination. An authentic "Down Under" bush jacket (about $25) that teams up perfectly with 100% brushed denim jeans (about $15) featuring the hip-trim, wide-flare "European Fit." Top them off with a Lee shirt (about $16) that's a waffle plaid in Blues, Browns and Greens. Do that and you've got another great Lee Jeans Suit going for you. The Lee Company...

Also in Sports

7th -21st Jun– The first ICC Cricket World Cup was held in England. It was the first major international tournament of One-Day Cricket. Eight nations participated with West Indies winning the cup.

6th Sep– Martina Navratilova defected from Czechoslovakia, seeking US political asylum in New York City during the US Open. At 18-years-old, the rising tennis star would become one of the greatest players of all time.

1st Oct– The third and final boxing match between the undisputed heavyweight champion Muhammad Ali, and former champion Joe Frazier, took place in the Philippines. Known as the *Thrilla in Manila*, the bout was conceded after fourteen rounds. Ali won 2-1 in what was regarded as one of the most brutal fights in boxing history.

3rd Nov– American Chris Evert became the first #1 ranked tennis player when the Women's Tennis Association introduced tour rankings. Evert would stay in the top spot for six months.

10th Apr– 41-year-old Lee Elder became the first Black golfer to play in the US Masters, considered the most prestigious event in golf. It was a milestone for a sport that had never been known for racial tolerance.

1975– Arthur Ashe became the first Black man to win Wimbledon, and Frank Robinson became the first African American baseball manager.

Advertisement

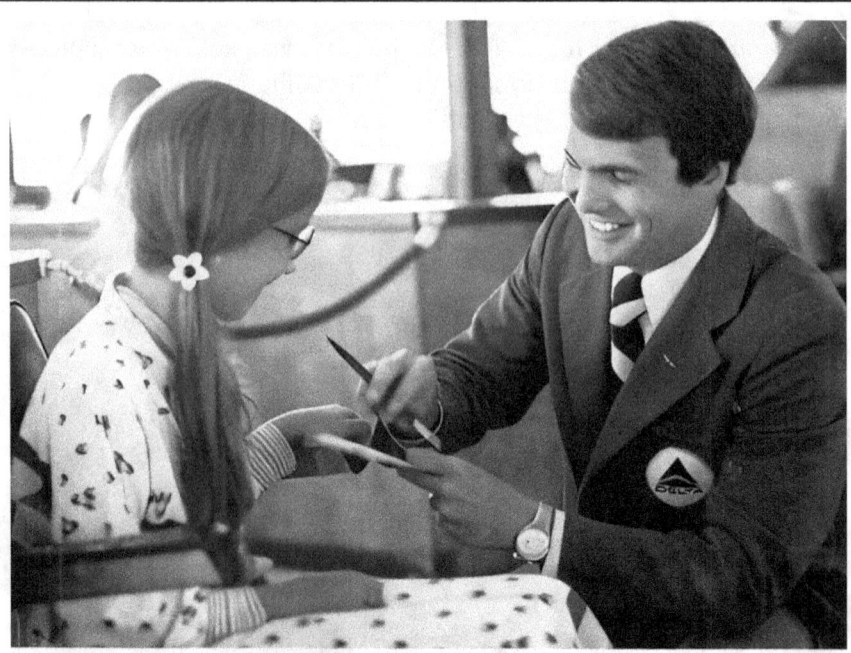

Delta is an air line run by professionals, like Tom Sineath. He has had a busy career with Delta. He's worked in cabin service, behind the ticket counter, at the boarding gate, handling many thousands of travelers.

Now Tom is a Delta Passenger Service Agent. And he's ready for anything. A bewildered tourist who speaks no English. A rock group with a ton of instruments. A 14-year-old who lost her purse with her ticket in it.

Tom's job is helping people get where they're going. And when it comes to people, Tom Sineath—like all the other 28,000 Delta professionals— couldn't care more.

Delta is ready when you are.

This is Delta's Wide-Ride™ L-1011 TriStar, an $18 million superjet. Cabins are almost 19 feet wide. All 250 seats are two-on-the-aisle.

Delta is an air line run by professionals, like Tom Sineath. He has had a busy career with Delta. He's worked in cabin service, behind the ticket counter, at the boarding gate, handling many thousands of travelers.

Now Tom is a Delta Passenger Service Agent. And he's ready for anything. A bewildered tourist who speaks no English. A rock group with a ton of instruments. A 14-year-old who lost her purse with her ticket in it.

Tom's job is helping people get where they're going. And when it comes to people, Tom Sineath—like all the other 28,000 Delta professionals—couldn't care more.

Delta is ready when you are.

In Technology

January– Altair 8800, the world's first microcomputer, was released by Micro Instrumentation and Telemetry Systems (MITS). It became the first commercially successful personal computer.

4th Apr– Bill Gates and Paul Allen formed Microsoft in Albuquerque, New Mexico, to develop and sell their Altair BASIC interpreter software. The software was for use on the Altair 8800 and would be distributed by MITS.

7th Jun– Japan's Sony introduced the first home videocassette recorder– the Betamax. Sales in the US began in November '75 for between $1,000 and $1,400.

30th Sep– HBO made television history, delivering the first live transmission via satellite by broadcasting the Ali vs Frazier *Thrilla in Manila* boxing match. The three-year-old company signed a six-year contract to utilize the communications satellite Satcom I. This made HBO the first successful, satellite-delivered pay cable service in the USA.

1975– Computer hobbyist Stephen Wozniak began working on the Apple 1 prototype, an 8-bit motherboard-only personal computer. He formed Apple Inc. with his friend, Steve Jobs, in 1976, bringing the Apple 1 to market in July 1976.

1975– Steven Sasson of Eastman Kodak developed the first self-contained digital camera. The images, at 100 × 100 pixels (0.01 megapixels), were digitally recorded onto a cassette tape, a process that took 23 seconds per image.

Other News from 1975

The original wooden "magic cube" prototype created by Ernő Rubik.

30th Jan– Ernő Rubik applied for a patent on his "Magic Cube", later known as the Rubik's cube.

25th Mar– King Faisal of Saudi Arabia was assassinated, shot at point blank range by his nephew, Prince Faisal. In June of the same year, the prince was beheaded in the public square, a traditional method of execution under Islamic law.

13th Apr– Battles between Christian and Muslim factions in the downtown area of Beirut spark the Lebanese Civil War, which would last 15 years and kill an estimated 150 thousand people. Up to one million people would flee Lebanon during the war years.

27th Aug– Former Emperor of Ethiopia, Haile Selassie, died in prison. Years later, documents would surface to prove he was murdered by the military rulers who had come to power one year earlier in a coup d'état. In March 1975, the military rulers nationalized all land under sweeping land reforms, and formally abolished the monarchy, adopting Marxism–Leninism as their official ideology.

5th Jun– Egypt reopened the Suez Canal, closed since 1967 during the Six Day War (between Isreal and a coalition of Arab States). From 1967 to 1975, political and physical battles around the Canal continued. Fourteen ships were stuck in the canal the entire eight years. Twelve of the ships were found too deteriorated to be salvaged.

8th Aug– Typhoon Nina caused The Banqiao Dam in China to collapse. 230,000 people died from dam's collapse, with a further 130,000 deaths caused by the typhoon and subsequent famine and disease.

14th Sep– Rembrandt's oil painting "The Night Watch", one of the most famous paintings of the Dutch Golden Age, was vandalized in Amsterdam's Rijksmuseum. It was slashed several times with a bread knife by an unemployed school teacher.

18th Sep– Long-time fugitive Patty Hearst was apprehended, charged with armed bank robbery and sentenced to seven years in prison. Hearst, heiress to a newspaper empire, had been kidnapped in early 1974 and forced to take part in the bank robbery. It is alleged she had been brainwashed and confined in a closet by her kidnappers. In 1979 her prison sentence would be commuted by President Carter, and she would be given a full pardon in 1982 by President Clinton.

11th Oct– Hillary Rodham and William Jefferson (Bill) Clinton were married during a small ceremony in their living room in Arkansas. A much bigger reception was held the same evening

21st Oct– Vietnam War veteran and Air Force Sergeant Leonard Matlovich was discharged after publicly declaring his homosexuality, openly challenging the ban against homosexuals in the US military. He became an outspoken activist for the gay community, appearing on the cover of *Time* Magazine, and winning an Air Force reinstatement in 1980.

20th Nov– Spanish dictator Francisco Franco died due to a heart attack. Franco had ruled with an iron grip from 1936-1975. Following his death, Spain transitioned to a democracy. On 22nd Nov, the monarchy was restored and Juan Carlos I was proclaimed King of Spain.

1975– Gilette introduced the first plastic disposable razor. The Trac II featured a cartridge system with replaceable blades.

Famous People Born in 1975

5th Jan– Bradley Cooper, American actor.

4th Feb– Natalie Imbruglia, Australian-British singer-songwriter.

22nd Feb– Drew Barrymore, American actress.

25th Feb– Chelsea Handler, American comedian & actress.

2nd Mar– Lee Sun-kyun, South Korean actor (d. 2023).

15th Mar– Eva Longoria, American actress.

15th Mar– will.i.am [William James Adams Jr.], American singer-songwriter, rapper, musician.

27th Mar– Fergie [Stacy Ann Ferguson], American pop singer (The Black Eyed Peas).

2nd Apr– Pedro Pascal, Chilean-American actor.

2nd May– David Beckham English soccer midfielder.

8th May– Enrique Iglesias Spanish singer-songwriter.

12th May– Jonah Lomu, New Zealand rugby union winger (d. 2015).

26th May– Lauryn Hill, American singer-songwriter.

27th May– Jamie Oliver, British chef & TV personality.

29th May– Melanie Brown, English singer & TV personality.

30th May– CeeLo Green [Thomas Callaway], American TV Personality, singer-songwriter, actor & record producer.

4th Jun– Angelina Jolie, American actress.

4th Jun– Russell Brand, English comedian & TV personality.

27th Jun– Tobey Maguire, American actor.

30th Jun– Ralf Schumacher, German Formula 1 race car driver.

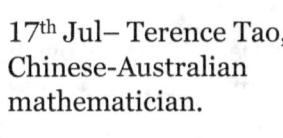
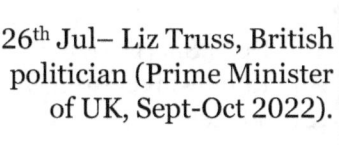

17th Jul– Terence Tao, Chinese-Australian mathematician.

26th Jul– Liz Truss, British politician (Prime Minister of UK, Sept-Oct 2022).

7th Aug– Charlize Theron,
South African actress.

12th Aug– Casey Affleck,
American actor.

16th Aug– Taika Waititi,
New Zealand film
director & actor.

9th Sep– Michael Bublé,
Canadian singer & actor.

18th Sep– Jason Sudeikis,
American comedian,
writer & actor.

30th Sep– Marion Cotillard,
French actress.

5th Oct– Kate Winslet,
British actress.

7th Oct– Tim Minchin,
Australian comedian
& musician.

22nd Oct– Jesse Tyler
Ferguson, American TV actor
& musical theatre performer.

17th Dec– Milla Jovovich,
Ukrainian-American actress.

18th Dec– Sia [Furler],
Australian singer-songwriter
& producer.

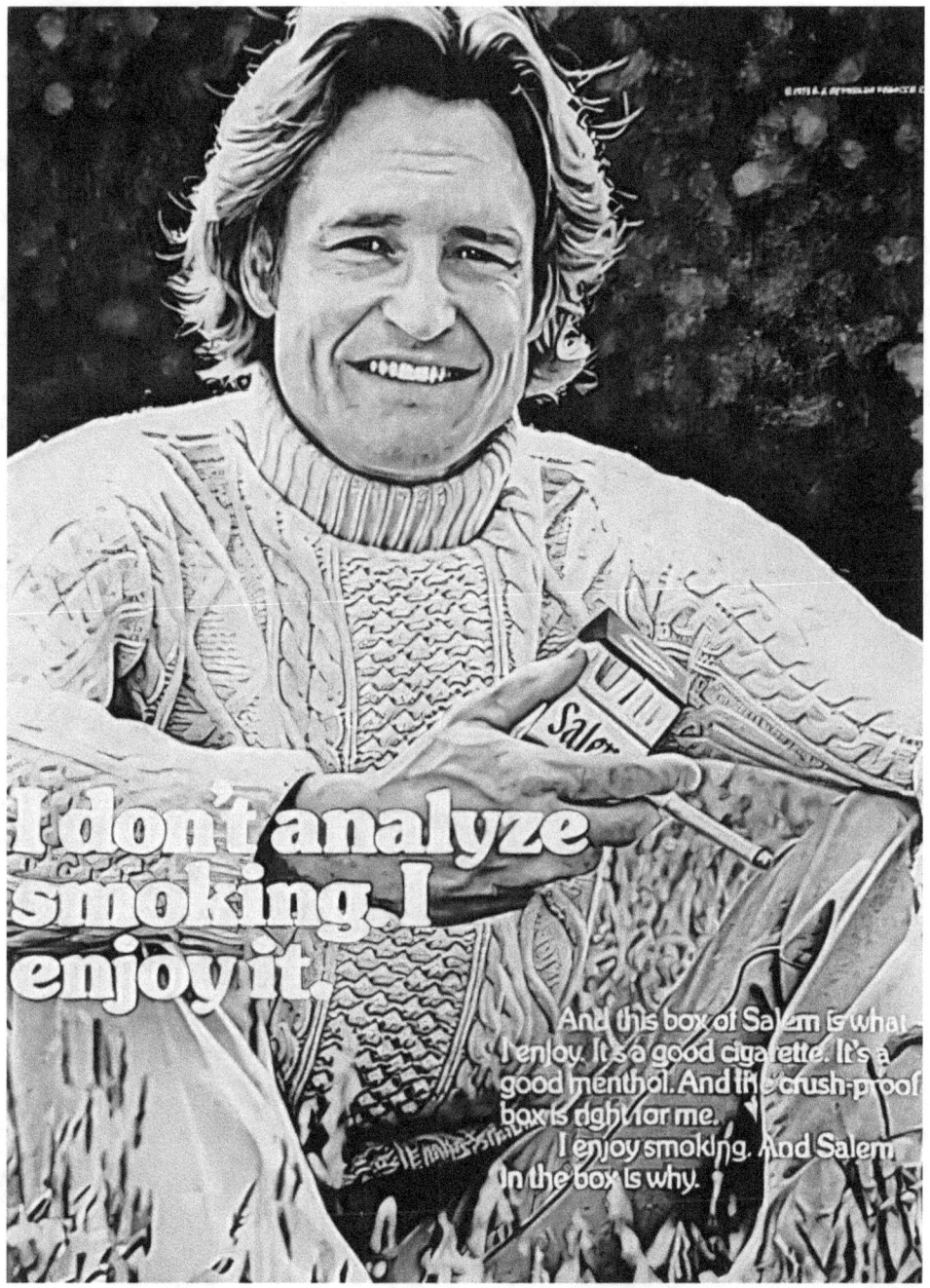

I don't analyze smoking. I enjoy it.
And this box of Salem is what I enjoy. It's a good cigarette. It's a good menthol. And the crush-proof box is right for me.
I enjoy smoking. And Salem in the box is why.

1975 in Numbers

Census Statistics [1]

- Population of the world   4.07 billion
- Population in the United States   219.13 million
- Population in the United Kingdom   56.22 million
- Population in Canada   23.15 million
- Population in Australia   13.89 million
- Average age for marriage of women   21.1 years old
- Average age for marriage of men   23.5 years old
- Median family income USA $13,720 / year
- Unemployment rate USA   8.2 %

Costs of Goods [2]

- Average new house $33,570
- Average new car $4,250
- A gallon of gasoline $0.72
- Bread $0.39 per 22 oz loaf
- Bacon $1.29 per pound
- Beef, sirloin steak $1.39 per pound
- Oranges, Florida $0.79 per 5 lb bag
- Potatoes $0.99 for 20 lb bag
- Mayonnaise, Kraft $0.69 per quart jar
- Onions $0.08 per pound
- Ham, cooked $0.79 per pound
- Ketchup, Heinz $0.59 per 26 oz bottle
- Mouthwash, Listerine $1.29 per 32 oz bottle
- Portable cassette recorder $22.99
- Cinema ticket $1.00

---

[1] Figures taken from worldometers.info/world-population, US National Center for Health Statistics, *Divorce and Divorce Rates* US (cdc.gov/nchs/data/series/sr_21/sr21_029.pdf) and United States Census Bureau, *Historical Marital Status Tables* (census.gov/data/tables/time-series/demo/families/marital.html).

[2] Figures from thepeoplehistory.com, mclib.info/reference/local-history & dqydj.com/historical-home-prices/.

Advertisement

Welcome to all the new front doors to Greyhound's America.

Welcome to all the new front doors to Greyhound's America.

Greyhound's America is out there waiting. America the beautiful. America up close, from sea to shining sea. It all begins at our new front doors. All the big bright, brand new Greyhound Terminals we're opening, every month. Our new terminals make going Greyhound even nicer than it's always been.

They're convenient. Completely modern. More comfortable than you could ever imagine. All because we believe that travel should be a beautiful experience from beginning to end. Every one of our new terminals has everything to make it happen. And every one of our new terminals includes a speedy Greyhound Package Express center. The smart, new way to get packages there on time instead of sometime.

So look for our exciting, new terminals. Our new front doors to Greyhound's America. They're places we proudly hail. We think you will too.

Go Greyhound and leave the driving to us.

The Imp Next Door

Meet the Imp: Imperial. It mixes so smoothly, you might never guess what it's up to.
But for breaking the ice, it's up to your highest expectations.
Try the Imp tonight, with someone you know.
Or borrow a cupful from someone you'd like to know better.

Imperial: the Imp.

A heartfelt plea from the author:

I sincerely hope you enjoyed reading this book and that it brought back many fond memories from the past.

Success as an author has become increasingly difficult with the proliferation of **AI generated** copycat books by unscrupulous sellers. They are clever enough to escape copyright action and use dark web tactics to secure paid-for **fake reviews**, something I would never do.

Hence I would like to ask you—I plead with you—the reader, to leave a star rating or review on Amazon. This helps make my book discoverable for new readers, and helps me to compete fairly against the devious copycats.

If this book was a gift to you, you can leave stars or a review on your own Amazon account, or you can ask the gift-giver or a family member to do this on your behalf.

I have enjoyed researching and writing this book for you and would greatly appreciate your feedback.

Best regards,
Bernard Bradforsand-Tyler.

Please leave a
book review/rating at:

https://bit.ly/1975-reviews

Or scan the QR code:

Flashback books make the perfect gift-
see the full range at

https://bit.ly/FlashbackSeries

Image Attributions

Photographs and images used in this book are reproduced courtesy of:

Page 6 – 1975 print magazine advertisement for Sony Stereo Cassette Deck (PD image).*
Page 8 – Washington march, 26th Apr 1975. Creator unknown. Source: flickr.com/photos/washington_area_spark/40571539763. Attribution CC BY-SA 2.0.
Page 9 – Palm Beach International Concert, May 1974. Pre-1978, no copyright mark (PD image).
Page 10 – 1975 print mag advert for Bell. Source: flickr.com/photos/nester/4178028437/ (PD image).*
Page 11 – College girls 1973 by Ed Uthman. Attribution CC BY-SA 2.0.
Source: en.wikipedia.org/wiki/Youth#/media/File: 1970sgirls.jpg. – Stafford and Leonov in Soyuz Orbital Module, 17th Jul 1975. Nasa PIA Number: ast-5-298. Source: nasa.gov/image-detail/amf-ast-5-298/. Photos this page are pre-1978, no copyright mark (PD image).
Page 12 – 1975 print magazine advertisement for Smith-Corona Typewriters (PD image).*
Page 13 – Tyneside street protest in 1974, unknown creator, from the ChronicleLive archive.
Source: chroniclelive.co.uk/news/history/gallery/tyneside-1974-new-byker-wall-21734884. Pre-1978, no copyright mark (PD image).
Page 14 – Women's march for abortion right to choose, 21st Jun 1975. Creator & source unknown.
– Boy crossing road, date and creator unknown. Images this page are pre-1978. Where images are not in the public domain, they are included here for information only under US fair use laws due to: 1- images are low resolution copies; 2- images do not devalue the ability of the copyright holders to profit from the original works in any way; 3- Images are too small to be used to make illegal copies for use in another book; 4- The images are relevant to the article created.
Page 15 – Glasgow rubbish strike, 1975, creator unknown. Source: glasgowlive.co.uk/news/history/glasgows-rubbish-strikes-1975-kicked-24877335. Pre-1978, no copyright mark (PD image). – Junior doctor's strike, 1975, creator unknown. Source: peopleshistorynhs.org/when-do-doctors-strikes-end-a-perspective-from-1975/. Pre-1978, no copyright mark (PD image).
Page 16 – 1975 print magazine advertisement for World Book (PD image).*
Page 17 – From *Readers Digest* magazine, Nov 1975 (PD image).*
Page 18 – Commune members, source: allthatsinteresting.com/hippie-communes.
– Commune members pose in front of a tipi, by John Olson from Life Magazine, 18th Jul 1969. Source: books.google.com/books?id =K08EAAAAMBAJ&printsec. Pre-1978, no copyright mark (PD image).
Page 19 – Tending to the fields, source: burlingtonfreepress.com/story/news/local/vermont/2015/07/24/vermont-remains-hippie-epicenter/30564907/, photo by Rebecca Lepkoff of Vermont Historical Society. – Geodesic dome, source: vpr.org/post/communes-hippie-invasion-and-how-1970s-changed-state#stream/0 by Kate Daloz. – Commune bus, source: allthatsinteresting.com/hippie-communes. All images this page are pre-1978, no copyright mark (PD image).
Page 20 – From *Time* magazine, 10th Feb 1975 (PD image).*
Page 21 – Friday afternoon traffic heading out of Atlanta, by Al Stephenson / AJC file. Source: ajc.com/lifestyles/flashback-photos-through-the-years-1951-1997/ByK7dbup2R66nM4TMIWX9O/.
– Waiting for gas, creator unknown, 1974.
Page 22 – Images taken from 1975 print magazine advertisements for Chevrolet Vega, Ford Mustang II Mach 1, and Chevrolet Chevy Chevette Hatchback, source: Ebay. (PD images).*
Page 23 – Images taken from 1975 print magazine advertisements for Datsun 710, Toyota Celica GT, and Volkswagen Rabbit Golf, source: Ebay. (PD images).*
Page 24 – 1975 print magazine advertisement for Dodge '75 Dart Special Edition (PD image).*
Page 25 – 1975 advert for Caprice Classic. Source: flickr.com/photos/nesster/4381214085/ (PD image).*
Page 26 – *All in the Family* screen still, 4th May 1971, by CBS Television.** Source: en.wikipedia.org/wiki/All_in_the_Family #/media/File: Archie_and_Lionel_All_in_the_Family_1971.JPG.
Page 27 – *Rhoda* publicity image by CBS, 1974.** Source: commons.wikimedia.org/wiki/Category: Rhoda. – *Happy Days* publicity image and screen still from the show by ABC, 1974.**
Source: commons.wikimedia.org/wiki/Category:Happy_Days.
Page 28 – From *Readers Digest* magazine, Dec 1975.
Source: flickr.com/photos/91591049@N00/34799772983/ (PD image).*
Page 29 – Publicity photo for *Welcome Back, Kotter* by ABC, 1975.** – Publicity photo for *One Day at a Time* by CBS, 1975.** – Publicity photo for *Wonder Woman* by ABC, 1975.** – Publicity photo for *Good Morning America* by ABC, 1976.**
Page 30 – 1975 print magazine advertisement for Sears Free Spirit bicycles (PD image).*
Page 31 – 1975 print magazine advertisement for Kodak Carousel Projector (PD image).*
Page 32 – PAVN troops crossing a river. Source: awm.gov.au/collection/C1223180, accession number P03056.002. - PAVN soldiers on top of a helicopter. Source: en.wikipedia.org/wiki/Battle_of_Ban_Me_Thuot. - South Vietnamese army convoy. Source: commons.wikimedia.org/wiki/File:ACAV_and_M48_Convoy_Vietnam_War.jpg. Image is work of a U.S. Army soldier or employee, as part of that person's official duties. (PD image).
Page 33 – Civilians fleeing from Da Nang, 29th Mar 1975, and Xuan Loc, 20th Apr 1975.
Source: en.wikipedia.org/wiki/Hue%E2%80%93Da_Nang_Campaign. – Parade of soldiers in Saigon, 30th Apr 1975. Images are pre-1978, no copyright mark (PD images).
Page 34 – Sea Stallions approach USS Midway during Operation Frequent Wind, 29th April 1975.
U.S. Navy photo from the USS Midway (CV-41). Author: USN. This file is a work of a sailor or employee of the U.S. Navy, taken or made as part of that person's official duties. As a work of the U.S. federal government, it is in the public domain in the United States.

– South Vietnamese refugees arrive on a U.S. Navy vessel during Operation Frequent Wind, 29th April 1975. Source: en.wikipedia.org/wiki/ Fall_of_Saigon. – South Vietnamese civilians outside the US embassy in Saigon. Source: en.wikipedia.org/wiki/Fall_of_Saigon.
Page 35 – All images are courtesy of the Documentation Center of Cambodia.
Source: ushmm.org/genocide-prevention/countries/cambodia/khmer-rouge-revolution, and ushmm.org/genocide-prevention/countries/cambodia/forced-labor-and-collectivization
Page 36 – From *Ebony* magazine, Jan 1975.
Source: books.google.com/books?id=6MwDAAAAMBAJ&printsec (PD image).*
Page 37 – *Operation Emery Baneberry* at Nevada Proving Grounds, 18th Dec 1970. – *Encelade,* Moruroa Atoll, French Polynesia, 1971. Photos this page by US Army and are in the public domain.
Page 38 – Images by NASA, source: en.wikipedia.org/wiki/Apollo%E2%80%93Soyuz (PD images).
Page 39 – Mercury's South Pole. Source: images-assets.nasa.gov/image/PIA02415/PIA02415~orig.jpg. NASA ID: PIA02415. – Viking 1 lander. Source: images-assets.nasa.gov/image/101-KSC-75P-12/101-KSC-75P-12~orig.jpg. NASA ID: 101-KSC-75P-12. (PD images).
Page 40 – 1975 print magazine advertisement for Eastman Kodak Company (PD image).*
Page 41 – 1975 print magazine advertisement for Pan Am (PD image).*
Page 42 & 43 – *Peace Wall* by Robin Kirk, 2008. Source: flickr.com/photos/rightsatduke/4595426547/. Attribution 4.0 International (CC BY 4.0). – Street scenes after IRA bombings, creators unknown.
– Republican arrests, creators unknown. Source: anphoblacht.com/contents/26282. Pre-1978, no copyright mark. Images are pre-1978. Where images are not in the public domain, they are included here for information only under US fair use laws due to due to: 1- images are low resolution copies; 2- images do not devalue the ability of the copyright holders to profit from the original works in any way; 3- Images are too small to be used to make illegal copies for use in another book; 4- The images are relevant to the article created.
Page 44 – 1975 print magazine advertisement for Polaroid Super Shooter (PD image).*
Page 45 – Creators unknown. Images this page are pre-1978. Where images are not in the public domain, they are included here for information only under US fair use laws due to: 1- images are low resolution copies; 2- images do not devalue the ability of the copyright holders to profit from the original works in any way; 3- Images are too small to be used to make illegal copies for use in another book; 4- The images are relevant to the article created.
Page 46 – 1975 print magazine advertisement for Honda (PD image).*
Page 47 – Screen still from One Flew Over the Cuckoo's nest.** – John Travolta in 1983. Source: commons.wikimedia.org/wiki/Category:John_Travolta (CC BY-SA 3.0).*
Page 48 – Film posters for the movies *Jaws* by Universal, 1975.**– *One Flew Over the Cuckoo's Nest* by United Artists, 1975.**– *The Return of the Pink Panther* by United Artists, 1975.**
Page 49 – Film posters for the movies *Airport 1975* by Universal Pictures, 1975.**
– *The Towering Inferno* by 20th Century Fox, Warner Bros, 1974.**– *Earthquake* by Universal Pictures, 1974.**– *The Hindenberg* by Universal Pictures, 1975.**
Page 50 – 1975 print magazine advertisement for Technics by Panasonic (PD image).*
Page 51 – From *Playboy* magazine, Oct 1975. Source: flickr.com/photos/91591049@N00/24251065495/ (PD image).*
Page 52 – Pink Floyd, circa 1973, creator unknown. – Bruce Springsteen live at Max's Kansas City, 31st Jan 1973, creator unknown. – Queen, still image taken from the music video of *Bohemian Rhapsody*, 1975. These images are included here for information only under US fair use laws due to: 1- images are low resolution copies; 2- images do not devalue the ability of the copyright holders to profit from the original works in any way; 3- Images are too small to be used to make illegal copies for use in another book; 4- The images are relevant to the article created.
Page 53 – Elton John from *The Cher Show*, CBS Television. Source: commons.wikimedia.org/wiki/ Category: Elton_John_in_1975. – The Bee Gees on *The Midnight Special*, NBC TV, 1973 Source: commons.wikimedia.org/wiki/ Category:Bee_ Gees. – Donna Summer publicity photo by Francesco Scavullo for Casablanca Records. Source: commons.wikimedia.org/wiki/Category:Donna_Summer_in_ 1974. Photos this page are pre-1978, no copyright marks (PD images).
Page 54 – David Bowie from AVRO's TopPop (Dutch TV) in 1974, source: commons.wikimedia.org/wiki/ David_Bowie. – The Eagles from the cover of Rolling Stone magazine, photo by Neal Preston, 1975.
– Publicity photo for Captain and Tennille from their TV show, 1976. Source: commons.wikimedia. org/wiki/File:Captain_and_tennille_1976.jpg. – Stevie Wonder by MoTown Records, 21st Aug 1973. Source: commons. wikimedia.org/wiki/Category:Stevie_ onder_in_1973. All photos this page are pre-1978, no copyright marks (PD images).
Page 55 – John Denver publicity photo for RCA records, 9th Aug 1973. Source: commons.wikimedia. org/wiki/Category: John_Denver. Pre-1978, no copyright mark (PD image). – Helen Reddy, publicity photo from The Carol Burnett Show, Oct 1973. Source: commons.wikimedia.org/wiki/Category:Helen_ Reddy_in_1973. Photos this page are pre-1978, no mark (PD images).
Page 56 – 1975 print magazine advertisement for Sony (PD image).*
Page 57 – Images from the original stage shows in 1975. Creators unknown. Pre-1978, no copyright mark (PD image).

Page 58 – 1975 print magazine advertisement for Wella Shampoo (PD image).*
Page 59 – Original book covers. Images shown here are courtesy of the publishing house. Where images are not in the public domain, they are included here for information only under US fair use laws due to due to: 1- images are low resolution copies; 2- images do not devalue the ability of the copyright holders to profit from the original works in any way; 3- Images are too small to be used to make illegal copies for use in another book; 4- The images are relevant to the article created.
Page 60 – Pants and skirt-suit, 1969, creator unknown. Pre-1978, (PD image).– Maxi-dress by YSL, Spring-Summer 1969. Source: minniemuse.com/articles/creative-connections/ patchwork. (PD image).
Page 61 – Elizabeth Taylor, source: instyle.com/celebrity/transformations/elizabeth-taylors-changing-looks. – Thea Porter dress, photographer Patrick Hunt, 1970. – Weipert and Burda fashion show, Apr 1972, photo by Friedrich Magnussen. Permission CC BY-SA 3.0 DE. – Mini dresses, sources: pinterest.com/pin/99782947967669796/ and retrospace.org/2011_01_01_archive.html unknown photographers. Pre-1978, no copyright mark (PD image).
Page 62 – Fashions from Sears Catalogs, Pre-1978, no copyright mark (PD image). – Hungarian singer Szűcs Judit wears embroidered denim. Source: commons.wikimedia.org/wiki/File:Szűcs_Judit_ énekesnő._Fortepan_88657.jpg. Licensed under the Creative Commons Attribution-Share Alike 3.0 Unported. – Knit polyester pants from the 1975 J.C. Penney catalog. Pre-1978, no copyright marks (PD image). – Flared jumpsuits, creator unknown. Pre-1978, no marks (PD image).
Page 63 – From *Playboy* magazine Oct 1975. Source: flickr.com/photos/91591049@N00/24142986742/ (PD image).*
Page 64 – Nik Nik shirts, polyester jumpsuits, and knit pantsuits, source: onedio.com/haber/erkekte-retro-modasinin-tutmamasinin-32-mantikli-sebebi-300983. – Polyester tops and pants, toweling jumpsuits, and shrink tops by Colombia Minerva, source: flashbak.com/the-good-the-bad-and-the-tacky-20-fashion-trends-of-the-1970s-26213/. – Denim on denim source: typesofjeanfits.com/a-brief-history-of-jeans-denim-history-timeline/. – Safari suits source: klyker.com/ 1970s-fashion/. All images this page Pre-1978, no copyright mark or renewal (PD image).
Page 65 – Still image from *Saturday Night Fever* by Paramount Pictures.** Source: vocal.media/beat/ the-list-saturday-night-fever-40th-anniversary. – Dancers Studio 54, sources: definition.org/ studio-54/2/ & alexilubomirski.com/image-collections/studio-54. Pre-1978, no copyright marks (PD image).
Page 66 – From *Playboy* magazine, Oct 1975. Source: flickr.com/photos/91591049@N00/24832451360/ in/photostream/ (PD image).*
Page 67 – Martina Navrátilová in 1980, by Hans van Dijk for Anefo. Source: commons.wikimedia.org/ wiki/Category:Martina_Navrátilová_in_1980. Pre-1978 (PD image). – Ali stuns Frazier in the 9th round, Thriller in Manila, 1st Oct 1975, by Mitsunori Chigita. Photo is included here for information only under US fair use laws due to: 1- image is low resolution copy; 2- image doe not devalue the ability of the copyright holder to profit from the original work in any way; 3- Image is too small to be used to make illegal copies for use in another book; 4- The image is relevant to the article created. – Chris Evert in Fort Lauderdale, Florida, 1975. Source: commons.wikimedia.org/wiki/Category:Chris_Evert (PD image).*
Page 68 – 1975 print magazine advertisement for Delta (PD image).*
Page 69 – All photos these pages are pre-1978 and are likely to be in the public domain. Where not in the public domain, they are included here for information only under US fair use laws due to: 1- images are low resolution copies; 2- images do not devalue the ability of the copyright holders to profit from the original works in any way; 3- Images are too small to be used to make illegal copies for use in another book; 4- The images are relevant to the article created.
Page 70 & 71– All photos these pages are pre-1978 and are likely to be in the public domain. Where not in the public domain, they are included here for information only under US fair use laws due to: 1- images are low resolution copies; 2- images do not devalue the ability of the copyright holders to profit from the original works in any way; 3- Images are too small to be used to make illegal copies for use in another book; 4- The images are relevant to the article created.
Pages 72-74– All photos are, where possible, CC BY 2.0 or PD images made available by the creator for free use including commercial use. Where commercial use photos are unavailable, photos are included here for information only under US fair use laws due to: 1- images are low resolution copies; 2- images do not devalue the ability of the copyright holders to profit from the original works in any way; 3- Images are too small to be used to make illegal copies for use in another book; 4- The images are relevant to the article created.
Page 75 – 1975 print magazine advertisement for Salem Cigarettes (PD image).*
Page 78 – From Ebony magazine, Jan 1975.
Source: https://books.google.com/books?id=6MwDAAAAMBAJ&printsec (PD image).*
Page 79 – 1975 print magazine advertisement for Charter Greyhound (PD image).*

*Advertisement (or image from an advertisement) is in the public domain because it was published in a collective work (such as a periodical issue) in the US between 1925 and 1977 and without a copyright notice specific to the advertisement.
**Posters for movies or events are either in the public domain (published in the US between 1925 and 1977 and without a copyright notice specific to the artwork) or owned by the production company, creator, or distributor of the movie or event. Posters, where not in the public domain, and screen stills from movies or TV shows, are reproduced here under USA Fair Use laws due to: 1- images are low resolution copies; 2- images do not devalue the ability of the copyright holders to profit from the original works in any way; 3- Images are too small to be used to make illegal copies for use in another book; 4- The images are relevant to the article created.

This book was written by Bernard Bradforsand-Tyler as part of *A Time Traveler's Guide* series of books.

All rights reserved. The author exerts the moral right to be identified as the author of the work.

No parts of this book may be reproduced, stored in any retrieval system, or transmitted in any form or by any means, without prior written permission from the author.

This is a work of nonfiction. No names have been changed, no events have been fabricated. The content of this book is provided as a source of information for the reader, however it is not meant as a substitute for direct expert opinion. Although the author has made every effort to ensure that the information in this book is correct at time of printing, and while this publication is designed to provide accurate information in regard to the subject matters covered, the author assumes no responsibility for errors, inaccuracies, omissions, or any other inconsistencies herein and hereby disclaims any liability to any party for any loss, damage, or disruption caused by errors or omissions.

All images contained herein are reproduced with the following permissions:
- Images included in the public domain.
- Images obtained under creative commons license.
- Images included under fair use terms.
- Images reproduced with owner's permission.

All image attributions and source credits are provided at the back of the book. All images are the property of their respective owners and are protected under international copyright laws.

First printed in 2024 in the USA (ISBN 978-1-922676-35-1).
Self-published by B. Bradforsand-Tyler.

www.ingramcontent.com/pod-product-compliance
Lightning Source LLC
Chambersburg PA
CBHW070321120526
44590CB00017B/2764